THE ADVENTURES OF DEBORAH AND KITE AT THE BIG RIVER

Gillian Blackah-Kingsley

Copyright © 2021 Gillian Blackah-Kingsley

ISBN: 978-1-7363499-0-8 (Paperback)

ISBN: 978-1-7363499-2-2 (Hardback)

ISBN: 978-1-7363499-1-5 (eBook)

Cover images and all illustrations by Nicola E. Hill

Edited by Anna Elkins

Book design by Barton Interactive, Redding, CA, USA

Printed by IngramSpark, in the United States of America

First Edition, 2021

Golden Flower Publishing

Author's Website: GillianBlackah-Kingsley.com

I am dedicating this book to my lovely husband and partner in life, Steve Kingsley ~

Thank you for your love and patience as the story took shape and for listening to me read it to you over and over again!

Thank you for your valuable wisdom and insight, and....

Thank you for always believing in me!

Thank you to my editor, Anna Elkins Sandeen, who did a wonderful job and was so kind and patient with me during the editing of this book.

Thank you to my gifted illustrator, artist Nicola Hill, who became a friend and prayer partner as we worked on the book together. Thank you for bringing the characters to life in such an endearing way.

Thank you to Zack, Katherine, and David at Barton Interactive who have done a superb job of formatting the book ready for printing. It was worth the wait!

Thank you all for your help with this project ~ I appreciate you so much and could not have done it without you!

"She believed she could, so she did."

~ R.S. GREY

PART 1

In Search of Golden Flowers

CHAPTER 1
Bluebell Meadows

This is the story of a most unusual yet wonderful friendship. After all, whoever heard of a honey bee and an eagle becoming the best of friends? But Deborah was no ordinary bee.

Deborah grew up in Bluebell Meadows, a quiet stretch of land at the edge of the Ancient Forest. Generations ago her family had built their nest in the hollow of an old oak tree, which had long been abandoned by a family of woodpeckers.

Deborah had always been an inquisitive young bee, curious about the world beyond the meadows. She never understood why all her relatives seemed quite content buzzing around Bluebell Meadows day after day, following the same old routine. There was a whole world out there waiting to be explored! Her mother, Queen Miriam, had so many royal duties that she hardly ever left the nest. Everybody worked so hard making honey that they had no time for anything else.

But Deborah was young and dreamed about seeing life beyond the colony—deep down she knew she was made for adventure!

Far away from Bluebell Meadows on the banks of the Big River, Kite, the young fledgling eagle, lived a very different kind of life. He was completely content with his life and surroundings, and if nothing at all ever changed, that was fine with him. He was an only-egg eagle, and each day his parents looked after his every need. He simply sat in the comfort of the royal nest in the highest canopy at the top of the tallest pine tree, waiting for his parents to bring his meals and clean up after him. From the comfort of his nest Kite had beautiful views of the fields and the river below. It was a wonderful place to live. He was a very content young eagle.

This is the story of how Deborah and Kite became friends, and how both their lives were about to change forever.

One sunny summer morning, while working in the meadows gathering nectar and pollen with the worker bees, Deborah made up her mind: Today is the day I will begin my great adventure!

It was time to explore the land beyond the borders of the colony and go in search of the golden flowers which only grew along a particular stretch of the Big River many miles away.

As a baby bee, Deborah loved to listen to her old aunts and uncles tell of a distant land full of beauty and wonder with fields full of golden flowers. She had always dreamed of finding these flowers and tasting their sweet nectar for herself. None of her living relatives had actually been to the Big River themselves. No, they had only heard about the special flowers that grew there through the stories passed down the generations. The only bee Deborah knew who had ever ventured to the Big River was Uncle Albert.

Yet whenever her relatives told stories of the Big River, they always gave a stern warning to the young bees, "Now listen carefully, little ones. As we've told you before, it is far, far too dangerous for a honey bee to fly all the way to the Big River. There are great dangers out there beyond our meadows. You are forbidden to ever fly so far from home. Remember what happened to Uncle Albert?"

No one ever said what actually happened to Uncle Albert. All Deborah knew was that he went missing when she was small and he never returned to the colony. He was sent out by his sister, the queen, to find the golden flowers and spy out the land at the Big River. No one ever saw him again. Queen Miriam felt guilty about allowing him to go on such a dangerous mission alone, even though he had begged her to send him. The loss of the queen's brother was painful for everyone. Once in a while the young bees would hear somebody say, "Poor Uncle Albert," as they shook their heads and sighed.

Deborah missed her uncle. He had always been fun to be around when she was growing up in the nursery. She especially loved his singing and remembered his cheerful songs very well—even though singing was strictly forbidden in the colony. Deborah never understood why. The elders had banned all singing a long time ago when her grandmother was their queen. They said it distracted the worker bees from the serious task of collecting nectar and producing honey. They said honey bees are far too busy to sing.

Uncle Albert was the only bee Deborah knew who broke the no-singing rule. He couldn't help himself; he loved to sing! He would visit the nursery as often as he could and sing over the growing bees. She would never forget the special song he taught her before he left when no one else was around.

Oh, how Deborah wanted the freedom to sing! Some days were just too dreary to go about her work in silence. She longed for a day when she would be free to sing at the top of her voice and not care who was listening! Today could be that day, thought the young princess.

And now, flying among the bluebells, moving casually from flower to flower, she sensed that this was her moment. When she reached the farthest corner of the meadow away from the busy nest, she looked around to make sure no one was watching. The bushes there marked the boundary line for every bee in the nest. No bee was allowed to go beyond this point.

Deborah doubted anyone would even miss her, there were so many other bees to gather the nectar. Anyway, she was certain she would be back before dark. And one day she would lead the entire colony to the Big River herself and become a hero! They would probably call her "the bravest bee in the colony." Her small wings buzzed with excitement at the thought.

Deborah glanced around the meadow one last time before making her final move. Her heart was beating wildly as she dived headfirst into the bushes. She pushed her way through the thick undergrowth and soon emerged on the other side. The open fields spread out before her and she soared up and away, crossing several meadows as quickly as she could. On and on she flew, above colorful flowers and lush green grassland where herds of cattle were grazing in the fields.

Everything around her was more beautiful than she could have imagined. She was on her way, flying free at last, far from the striving and busyness of the colony at Bluebell Meadows. Deborah's heart was full of joy.

After a while it dawned on her that she was now free to sing out loud! The rules of the colony could no longer stop her. It had been a long time since the young princess had sung a song, so she took a deep breath and cleared her throat. Then she began to sing the song Uncle Albert taught her in the royal nursery when she was little. The words and the tune always made her happy.

Sweet and runny honey days in
fields of flowers and trees,
Sunny days are honey days in the
life of busy bees.

Buzzy bees are busy bees, making
honey for our friends,
Golden yellow, sweet and yummy,
every bee loves runny honey!

Runny honey is the best; it's sticky
and it's sweet,
It makes us strong to sing our song—
pure honey is a treat!

She laughed out loud for joy and sang her simple song over and over again as she flew toward the Big River.

After flying and singing for a long time, Deborah decided to rest for a moment and get her bearings. She knew the general direction of the Big River—everyone knew that—but she'd been traveling for quite some time now, and there was still no sign of water. She landed on a leaf and caught her breath.

Then Deborah looked up and saw her—the most beautiful creature she had ever seen.

CHAPTER 2
Emeth

Her large wings were bright and colorful and seemed to glow with flowing blues and yellowy-orange shades that were somehow alive. She was breathtaking! Deborah just had to meet this glorious butterfly.

She flew over to the long-stemmed flower where the lovely creature was feeding and said politely, "Hello-o-o there! My name is Deborah. I couldn't help noticing your beautiful wings, so colorful as they catch the sunlight. May I ask, what is your name?"

The heavenly creature pulled her head out of the flower, and replied warmly, "Oh, hello! Why thank you, Deborah. My name is Emeth, and it's a pleasure to meet you." Her voice was like music. As she spoke she fluttered her colorful wings.

Deborah was soon to discover that Emeth was a very kind butterfly indeed.

"I don't think I've ever seen you in this meadow before, Deborah. Are you lost?" she asked with concern.

"Oh, no, no, no, I'm not lost!" said Deborah confidently, "I just don't know exactly where I am... um, perhaps you can direct me to the Big River, please? I'm on an adventure, you see, to find the golden flowers. I hear they are tall and beautiful and have the most delicious nectar. I would like to take some back to my family at Bluebell Meadows. Have you heard of these flowers?"

"Ah yes, I know them well. They can only be found in the pastures where the sheep come to rest and drink. You are right—they have the best nectar. It's one of my favorite places to eat. Come with me; I'll be glad to show you the way!" And with one flap of her long, elegant wings Emeth floated up above Deborah's head and flew away in an explosion of color.

Deborah was delighted to have met such a helpful, friendly guide. She gladly followed, her much smaller wings buzzing as fast as they could to keep up with Emeth, who was surprisingly quick.

Deborah and her companion chatted easily as they flew over the countryside that afternoon, both enjoying their new friendship. It was like they had known each other all their lives.

They were having such a good time, in fact, that it didn't seem long at all before the Big River came into view.

"There it is!" Deborah exclaimed with delight.

The river looked like a deep blue ribbon, slowly winding its way through the grassy land below. It was even more beautiful than Deborah had imagined it in her dreams. It looked alive! The sun was dancing on the water, making it sparkle and gleam like tiny diamonds catching the light. It took her breath away.

Emeth smiled and followed as Deborah headed down toward the riverbank, buzzing her wings faster and faster. The young bee could see the pasture with a small flock of woolly white sheep lying down by the edge of the water, content and full from their grazing. And the fields were full of golden flowers! They seemed to be welcoming her, their faces turned toward the sun. She could hardly believe she was here at last!

"Ba-a-a, Ba-a-a... Ba-a-a-a-a!" was the sound which floated up to Deborah and Emeth as they got closer and closer and the Big River got bigger and bigger.

Oh, the joy Deborah felt as she followed Emeth down to the pasture, ready to feast on these glorious flowers! She could not wait to taste their goodness for herself.

CHAPTER 3
Flying Lessons

Meanwhile, high up in the tallest pine tree on the opposite side of the river, Kite, the young fledgling eagle, was reluctantly trying out his wings on a branch beyond the nest. This was a very dangerous thing to do in his opinion. He didn't see why he needed to learn how to fly anyway. He liked his home in the nest. It suited him very well. It was safe, warm, and comfortable, and his parents gave him everything he needed. He had no desire to leave at all.

But his father, the great eagle king, had told him that afternoon, "Kite, my son, we love you very much, but your mother and I feel it's now time for you to spread your wings and leave the nest. This means you must learn how to fly and how to feed yourself. You need to go and explore the land and one day find your future bride. Then together you will make a kingdom of your own along the Big River."

Trying not to look down, Kite answered, "But Papa, I don't want to leave, I'm not ready. And I don't like heights. I feel much safer here with you and Mother. You are always here to look after me. Please, can't I stay?"

The eagle king remembered his first flight from the highest branch of the tallest tree many years ago. At first, he hadn't felt ready either. But when he finally found the courage to try his wings, with his father by his side, he quickly learned that flying was a lot of fun. Once he had mastered the flying skills his parents taught him, he wanted to stay in the air forever! He knew that Kite would feel the same if he could only overcome his fear of heights.

The eagle king was a wise father. He told Kite, "My son, it is time for me to teach you about flying so you can experience the true life of an eagle. Not only is it dangerous for you to stay in the nest, Kite, but if you do not learn to fly, you will not become who you are created to be. You are a mighty eagle from a long line of mighty eagles. I must teach you all I know because one day you will rule and reign in the skies over this land."

And now here Kite was, reluctantly edging his way along the branch toward his father who was encouraging him with every step he took away from the comfort of the nest.

His father urged him, "You can do this, Kite. I'm right here. You were born to fly high above the trees and mountains!"

However, Kite was really, really afraid of heights. He could hardly focus on anything his father was telling him as fear gripped his heart. The eagle king could see his son was struggling, so he inched his large body along the branch to be closer to Kite and give him courage. Kite felt a lot better when his father was near, and he began to relax a little.

The eagle king then spread his huge wings and began to jump up and down on the branch to show Kite how to prepare for his first flight. However, the demonstration came without warning, and the king almost knocked the fledgling off his perch as he flapped his great wings.

"Now you try it, Kite!" his father said, as he continued to jump up and down. "Spread your wings like this and let your feet leave the branch. Go on son, jump and flap, jump and flap. You can do it!"

Very cautiously Kite opened his wings as wide as he could and jumped a timid little jump up and down with his eyes tightly closed. His proud father was so thrilled at the sight of his son taking his first ever "jump and flap" that he leapt up and down in excitement all the more.

"Great work, my son! Great work! That's right, like this!"

With both large birds jumping and flapping, the branch was bouncing so much that Kite suddenly lost his balance. His feet missed the branch, his body lurched forward and he tumbled head-first in a most spectacular dive.

He let out a loud screech as he plummeted down through the branches of the tree.

His father called out, "Spread your wings, Kite! Spread your wings and glide to the next branch!" But the young eagle was now falling faster and faster.

"He-l-l-l-p! Papa, help me!" Kite tried to open his wings and glide, but he was frozen with fear. His wings didn't seem to be working. It was all happening so quickly. Down, down, down he went, crashing through the tree.

CHAPTER 4
Sunflowers and Eagles

On the other side of the river, Deborah was having a wonderful time. To be in this honey bee paradise was a dream come true. The young princess was not disappointed; golden flowers grew everywhere! They were taller and more beautiful than any other flower she had ever seen. Their huge yellow faces tilted upward to soak up the rays of sun as it moved throughout the day.

As Deborah collected nectar from one giant flower face to the next, she thought, "I'm going to call these special flowers 'sunflowers' because they love the sun so much. They even look like the sun!" She ate and ate until her tummy was full and she could eat no more.

Emeth was still flitting around the meadow nearby, so Deborah decided to rest for a while in the center of a large sunflower by the water's edge.

As she was relaxing and enjoying the scenery, something she had never experienced before began to happen. Suddenly, she felt a strong passion to sing begin to stir in her, bubbling up from deep inside. This was different than earlier when she sang her uncle's song after leaving Bluebell Meadows. This was a deep desire from within, which was very unexpected.

She looked around, surprised by this new sensation. Had something happened to cause this feeling? Nothing had changed in the meadows. The other insects and birds were going about their day as usual. Yet something new was stirring inside her. In fact, this urge to sing seemed to be flowing up through the flower itself! She couldn't explain it. Even though she could not hear anything, it felt as if the sunflowers were inviting her to join their chorus!

At that moment Emeth arrived, joining her on the flower. Deborah's passion to sing faded away as quickly as it came.

Deborah didn't know what to make of the experience, but it felt like something had been awakened in her by these special flowers—something she didn't expect at all. Perhaps the rich sunflower nectar she'd been eating was having a strange effect on her.

The young bee decided she wouldn't even try to explain this unusual experience to Emeth. Instead, she turned her full attention to the butterfly who was a wonderful and interesting companion. Deborah wanted to find out more about her new friend.

So, as they sat together on the sunflower, Emeth shared her life story with Deborah. She explained that she was not born as a butterfly at all but came from her egg as a leaf-eating caterpillar. Then one day, hidden under a leaf in the secret place of her cocoon, she fell asleep and was magically transformed into a completely new creature. At just the right time, she was reborn and emerged as the butterfly she now was. The caterpillar was gone! Since then, she didn't even remember her old life. She lived each day in complete freedom to dance on the breeze and be who she was created to be.

Oh, how Deborah wished she could be free like Emeth. She thought her friend's life story was simply magical.

Suddenly, the peaceful afternoon was pierced by a high-pitched screech that jolted Emeth and Deborah from their conversation. This terrible scream was followed by the sound of branches cracking and twigs breaking. It was coming from a huge pine tree across the river. Emeth and Deborah watched in amazement as a large brown bird appeared about halfway down the tree, dangling upside down from a branch by its feet!

The butterfly and bee looked at each other, then back again at this strange sight. Without saying a word the friends flew together across the river toward the tree to investigate. As they got closer, dodging the leaves and small twigs still falling from above where the poor bird was hanging, they could see it was a young eagle. He had clearly fallen headfirst from a great height, probably while trying to fly for the first time.

Kite was very shaken. He was also very embarrassed. Here he was upside down, clinging to a branch for dear life. Kite felt humiliated. How was he ever going to get back to the nest from here?

No one could help him. He got into this mess and he would have to get himself out of it.

The blood was rushing to his head, and he thought he saw a brightly colored butterfly and a small bee flying toward him. Kite's wings flapped slowly in dismay.

"Oh no, now I'm seeing things!" he thought.

Deborah buzzed toward him and said brightly, "Hi there! It looks like you had quite a fall. What's your name?"

Kite thought, "Oh dear, I must be hearing things too. It sounds like that bee is talking to me."

Out loud he said, "Umm... my name is Kite." After all, he didn't want to be rude.

"Very nice to meet you, Kite. My name is Deborah. I'm on an adventure this afternoon all the way from Bluebell Meadows and this is my guide and new friend, Emeth. We saw you from across the river over there and came to see if we can help you. You look like you could do with a little help." Deborah landed on a leaf close by Kite's upside-down head and smiled kindly at the unfortunate bird.

Kite stopped mid-flap. His eyes grew bigger. How could this tiny insect with miniature wings think it could help a big, clumsy bird who was hanging from his feet halfway down the tallest tree in the land? But he kept his thoughts to himself.

Instead he said patiently, "Nice to meet you both. I haven't learned to fly yet. I just fell from all the way up there." He moved his big head up to point toward the top of the tree. "I don't like heights, you see."

An eagle who doesn't like heights! Deborah thought this was the funniest thing she had ever heard. In fact, she was about to laugh out loud when Emeth cleared her throat loudly as if to say, "Do not laugh at him in his condition."

So instead Deborah giggled on the inside and said, "You don't like heights? But you're an eagle, right?"

Kite felt very foolish and sighed a deep sigh. "Yes, I am an eagle. My father is the great eagle king. We live at the top of this tree. He was teaching me how to fly, and this is where I ended up. I felt so afraid when we were jumping and flapping that I lost my balance on the branch. Instead of gliding like he told me to, I fell headfirst down here."

Kite looked discouraged, and his wings were now still.

"Don't worry, Kite," Emeth said cheerfully as she fluttered around him, looking for any damage from the fall, "You just need to know who you are, that's all. Once you start to believe in yourself, you'll realize that you were made to fly, and you'll soon be flying high, being who you were made to be! There is nothing better than that in this world." She smiled kindly, feeling sorry for the discouraged bird.

This was true, but Deborah and Emeth could see that Kite did not believe in himself yet—and that was the real problem.

Kite remained quiet and still. He was feeling quite sorry for himself. How would he ever learn to fly with such a fear of heights? Who was he created to be anyway? He was a bird; yes, an eagle.

He liked his life in the nest where he felt safe and secure. But Emeth was right. He didn't know what it was like to fly high and free like the other birds.

Deborah broke into his thoughts with a bright idea.

"I know how we can help you! Emeth and I will simply stay here with you until you are ready to let go of that branch, trust those great big wings of yours, and glide away from this tree. We believe in you, Kite. We know you can do this!"

Emeth agreed, "That's right. We won't leave you. We're your friends now and we'll do this together. We are here for you for as long as it takes. How does that sound to you?"

Suddenly, as Kite was thinking about how to answer, out of nowhere two large black-and-white birds came crashing through the foliage and landed heavily on the branch right above Kite's feet. While the birds flapped their wings wildly, making a commotion, Emeth and Deborah hid behind a thick covering of leaves and twigs, unnoticed by the intruders. The two friends kept out of sight, not knowing what would happen next.

The black-eyed magpies were laughing mercilessly at the unfortunate young eagle hanging below them. They had been flying down the river when they heard the loud screech. Turning around to investigate, they spotted Kite hanging from the branch. These bully birds couldn't resist the opportunity to make fun of a helpless victim, especially the future king of the skies.

Kite had met these mean scavengers once before. Some time ago the magpie twins had appeared at the top of his tree. The birds had flown in circles above the eagles' nest, mocking him as he sat there unable to fly or defend himself. Fortunately, the eagle king had returned to feed Kite his breakfast and chased them away, telling them never to come back.

But now they were back, and the eagle king was nowhere to be seen.

CHAPTER 5
The Bully Birds

The black-and-white brothers were thoroughly enjoying the sight before them. Here was the eagle king's precious son, the "prince of the great tree," the heir to the kingdom of the skies, clinging to a branch upside down! Hah! Now they could really have some fun.

"Just hanging around, are you? Haha!" one of them jeered, laughing loudly at his own joke. "Where's your daddy when you need him? There's no one here to protect you now, is there?" They sneered, enjoying a sense of power over the unfortunate bird, who was easily twice their size.

"You call yourself an eagle? You failed your flying test, didn't you? You can't even fly. You look more like a bat hanging there! I know, we're going to call you the Bat Eagle from now on."

The two bully birds started squawking loudly, shouting, "Bat Eagle, Bat Eagle, you can't fly-y-y! Bat Eagle, Bat Eagle we know why-y-y!"

The beady-eyed brothers kept up their cruel game, jumping around from branch to branch. Although they appeared confident, the magpies kept looking over their shoulders just in case Kite's father appeared. They knew they were no match for the eagle king.

As he hung there listening to their insults, Kite's thoughts went to his new friends, Deborah and Emeth. Where were they? He hoped they were somewhere safe because they were in real danger from these birds who would not think twice about eating them for supper.

Up until that moment, the magpie twins had not noticed Emeth and Deborah, who were hiding back in the foliage. But Emeth's wings were so bright and colorful in the late afternoon sunlight that when she moved even slightly, one of the beady-eyed brothers caught sight of her among the green pine needles.

"Oh look! What do we have here?" asked one of the birds, peering into the branches to get a closer look at the butterfly and her companion.

"Well, what do you know? It looks to me like a bee and a butterfly hiding back there! A tasty insect snack, for sure. Which one do you want, Bro'? I think I'm in the mood for a sweet honey-flavored snack myself." He snapped his beak open and closed a few times at the thought of an easy meal.

"Okay, then I'll have the one with the floaty wings. I like wings for supper!" They cackled and danced around from branch to branch, feeling pleased with themselves. It seemed they had

Emeth and Deborah trapped in the tree.

The magpies moved in closer to try and flush out the frightened friends from their hiding place right above the branch where Kite was hanging. The birds' beaks were frantically snapping together as they started pulling away the tangle of twigs and small branches to grab their prize.

Kite knew he had to do something—and quickly! Forgetting his fear, he began to swing his large body up toward the magpies who were fully focused on their victims. He swayed back and forth a few times then swung up with all his strength, let go of the branch, and aimed for the black-and-white bullies. He spread his great wings wide and slammed into them with full force, knocking the brothers off their perch into mid-air! They were completely caught off guard by the young eagle's power and strength. Squawking loudly, they fled from the tree in a panic as fast as they could, leaving several black-and-white feathers behind.

Deborah and Emeth were safe—but Kite wasn't. Once he had let go of the tree, Kite started heading in the wrong direction: down, down, down, toward the river! He was falling fast and was about to plunge headfirst into the deep waters when he remembered to keep his wings wide and glide as his father had taught him. Just before he hit the river's surface, he managed to pull himself up and began to rise, his feet skimming the water.

He did it! He soared up and up, feeling the wind under his wings, flying for the very first time. At that same moment, the eagle king appeared out of nowhere flying underneath his son, calling out, "Well done, Kite! You did it—you're flying! I am so proud of you. I knew you could do it!"

"Papa! I can fly!" Kite looked at his father, amazed that they were flying together over the water. Kite was relieved to see the eagle king. He was thrilled to be flying but was still shaken up by what had just happened.

His father told him, "I saw you hanging in the tree, son, and I was ready to come to your rescue if you needed me. But I knew you would overcome your fear of heights—those menacing magpies didn't stand a chance!"

"Thanks, Papa. I think I'm going to need a lot more practice—and I'm not too sure how I'm going to land!" Kite replied, still feeling wobbly.

The eagle king assured him, "Don't worry, you will get the hang of it. It will become as natural as breathing in no time. It's what you were born to do!"

They flew together over the fields and trees so Kite could get used to his wings and gain some confidence. But it wasn't long before the young eagle's thoughts returned to his new friends. What had happened to Deborah and Emeth?

"Papa, I need to go find my friends and make sure they're safe. I'll be okay flying alone, I promise!" The king nodded his approval as Kite circled back to the tree where he had last seen them.

Kite spotted a firm-looking branch and prepared for his first tree landing. "How difficult can it be?" he thought to himself as he approached his target. But he was flying way too fast and missed the branch completely. He circled back around to try again. On his third attempt, Kite slowed down enough and his timing was perfect. He managed to connect his feet to the branch and made his first successful landing.

He searched the tree, calling out to Deborah and Emeth, but there was no sign of them anywhere. What if those mean birds had come back and... no, he would not think about that now. He would keep looking until he found them. Gathering his courage Kite launched off the branch and glided down toward the pasture where the sheep were grazing on the other side of the river. He searched the meadows, his sharp eagle eyes sweeping the land below for any sign of them.

He must find out what had happened to his new friends.

CHAPTER 6
Meeting a True King

After the magpie brothers had fled the tree, Deborah and Emeth were feeling shaken by the experience with the bullies. But they were both in awe of the young eagle who had saved their lives. As they emerged from their hiding place, Deborah said to Emeth,

"Wasn't Kite amazing the way he knocked those black-eyed bandits off the tree to save us? I knew he could do it—I knew he could let go of that branch!"

"Yes, it was spectacular how he came to our rescue," Emeth agreed. "Come on, Deborah, let's go down by the water's edge and wait for Kite where he can see us. I'm sure he will be looking for us by now."

The magpies were nowhere to be seen, so the two friends flew down from the tree and settled on a small rock in the shade at the river's edge. The sheep were grazing nearby and it was quiet and peaceful. They took a long, refreshing drink from the river. What an adventure this was turning out to be!

They didn't have to wait long for Kite. Having circled around the meadows a few more times, the young eagle was relieved to see his friends resting by the shallows and flew down to join them. But having never landed on the ground before, he miscalculated his speed and approached far too fast. Wings, feet, and feathers came hurtling down out of the sky. With a huge thump, Kite landed heavily on the grass close by, sending startled sheep running in all directions.

Still sprawled out on the grass with his feet in the air, he lifted his big head and said, "Am I glad to see you two! I was getting worried. Did those mean birds hurt you?" He seemed more concerned about his friends than he was for himself.

Deborah and Emeth were relieved to see he was not injured. "Hello, Kite! Thanks for dropping in!" Deborah joked, flying over to greet him as he picked himself up from the crash landing.

"We are both fine, thanks to you. Thank you so much for what you did back there in the tree. Those birds were going to eat us for supper! You put yourself in danger to save us, and that was very brave of you."

Emeth flapped her colorful wings. "Yes, Kite, we cannot thank you enough for what you did. Those cowardly bullies didn't stand a chance!"

Kite smiled, stood up tall, and shook himself. "You're welcome. I couldn't let those mean birds eat my new friends! To be honest, I didn't have much time to think about it; it happened so fast. I even surprised myself when I finally let go of the branch!" They all laughed, relieved to be back together and in one piece.

Deborah buzzed around him. "It looks like your first flight was a great success, Kite—and you overcame your fear of heights. We knew you could do it; well done!"

"Thank you! I need more landing practice though; crash landings are really painful!" He chuckled, smoothing his ruffled feathers.

Just then, Kite's father arrived, gliding down to a large rock at the edge of the river. Deborah and Emeth were in awe of the eagle king's beauty and majesty. His great white head and deep brown body cast a long shadow in the sunlight. They had never met a true king before.

"Papa, let me introduce my new friends, Deborah and Emeth. They came to help me when they saw me hanging in the tree. They stayed with me when I was afraid, and it was their belief in me that helped me to eventually let go of the branch," Kite said proudly.

"Is that so?" The king said kindly, looking at the two friends. "Well, it's a great pleasure to meet you both. Thank you for helping my son overcome his fear. Your actions showed great compassion and bravery."

"Sir, I mean, Your Majesty, how were we brave? We didn't really do anything," Deborah replied.

"Oh, but it sounds like you did, my dear. You saw Kite in need of a friend and did something about it. Those cowardly birds came to bully him, but you came to encourage a young bird who was a stranger to you. You helped him to find the courage to fly. You saw who Kite really is when he could not see it in himself—and that is true friendship."

"Thank you, Your Majesty," replied Deborah, "I'm glad we were there and could help your son. But we want you to know that Kite is the true hero."

They all turned to look at the young eagle as Deborah continued, "The magpies spotted us hiding back in the tree and were trying to eat us. Kite saved our lives today."

The eagle king turned to his son. "Is this true that you let go of the branch in order to save your friends?"

"Yes, Papa. I had to do something."

Kite's father could not have been more proud of his son's brave actions to face his fear and help his friends. "You showed great courage today, son. I am very proud of you," he said.

The king turned to Deborah and Emeth. "You must come to our home to meet Kite's mother. The eagle queen will want to thank you personally for helping Kite find his wings and fly."

Emeth spoke first, "Thank you for your kind offer, Your Majesty. It has been wonderful to meet you all today, and I know we will meet again. But now I must say goodbye. It's getting late and my family will be worried about me."

Kite and his father bowed their heads to honor Emeth as she stretched out her beautiful wings, ready for her journey home.

She turned to her new friend. "Deborah, I am so glad we met this afternoon and became friends. Thank you for including me in your adventure."

"Yes, of course, and thank you for being such a wonderful guide!" Deborah exclaimed, "I do hope we will meet again soon. But before you go, I've been wanting to ask you one question. Please will you tell us what your beautiful name means?"

"It means 'Truth,'" Emeth answered. And with that, she flew up and away, leaving a trail of sparkling colors and magical beauty in the fading sunlight. They watched in wonder until she disappeared from view.

"Son, it's time to go now," said the eagle king. "It's getting late and your mother will be waiting for us."

Kite asked Deborah, "Won't you come with us? Please? It's a long way back to your family, and it's almost dark. You are welcome to stay the night in our nest where it's safe and warm. I will gladly fly you back to your home tomorrow at first light. After all, I need the flying practice!" he said with laughter in his eyes.

Deborah didn't know what to say to this most generous offer. She looked at Kite's father.

He smiled warmly and said, "Yes, I insist, you must come and stay with us. We would be honored to have you in our home."

"Well then, yes! I would love to accept your kind offer," Deborah said with delight. Her wings buzzed loudly as they always did when she was excited.

She could not have imagined a more perfect end to the day. Invited to stay in the royal nest for the night... wowee! Her family and friends wouldn't believe her when she told them about this incredible day!

Kite lowered his wing to her. "Climb up on my back and hold on tight. Off we go!"

Up they went, the eagle king flying beneath Kite to give him extra confidence as he rose up high toward the top of the pine tree.

The queen was in the nest waiting for them. She was pleased to welcome Deborah and was extremely proud of Kite as he told her what had happened that afternoon.

As his mother smoothed her son's feathers she said, "You know, son, your father was never far away from you today. His eyes were on you the whole time, and he was ready to help you if you had needed him. But you knew just what to do, and we are both very proud of you."

Darkness fell as they settled down in the nest for the evening. Deborah felt very sleepy, but before she could rest, she had to know the answer to one question. As quietly as she could, she flew across the nest and landed close to the eagle king's white head. The great bird was still awake and seemed to be deep in thought, as kings often are.

"Excuse me, Your Majesty, may I speak with you for a moment?"

The king nodded.

"I am curious why you chose not to help Kite this afternoon when the magpie brothers were bullying him. How did you know he would be able to handle them on his own?" Deborah asked.

"Ah, yes. That is a good question, Deborah, and one that is easy for me to answer. You see, Kite is from a long line of kings. I've watched him grow stronger and stronger each day since he was born. He has royal blood in his veins and the heart of a good king. It was important for him to discover his own strength in the face of danger. I knew he would know what to do. The truth is, your belief in him today and your friendship was all he needed for his fear to turn into courage."

The king's wise words filled Deborah's heart.

"Thank you, Your Majesty. You have raised a kind and brave son. Goodnight to you." She flew back across the nest to Kite's side.

What a day! When she left Bluebell Meadows that morning, she could not have imagined her grand adventure would end so perfectly. She and Emeth had helped a young eagle overcome fear to become a true prince.

"Goodnight, Kite," she whispered, aware that he was already asleep. Deborah slept soundly, tucked safely under Kite's wing.

CHAPTER 7
The Surprising Discovery

Early the next morning, Deborah woke to the sound of cheerful birdsong echoing around the Big River. Every bird living in the great tree, large and small, joined in the dawn chorus.

Deborah poked her head out from beneath Kite's warm feathers and flew to the edge of the nest. It had been getting dark when they arrived last night, and Deborah had no idea how high above the river she was until this moment. What an incredible view!

"Isn't this a wonderful place to live?" said Kite as he joined her.

"Yes, indeed it is. I have never been so high up in all my life! Even the Big River looks small from up here."

Kite chuckled at his new friend as her small wings hummed loudly. As they were enjoying the view together, Kite suddenly remembered that Deborah was not the first bee he had ever met. He told her the story.

"One day, when I was alone in the nest waiting for my parents to come back from fishing, I heard a sound like singing. But it wasn't a bird singing like the birds this morning. It was different. I couldn't understand where it was coming from, so I went to the edge of the nest to look.

"Suddenly, a honey bee appeared out of nowhere and landed right next to me! He was an older bee who was quite out of breath. He seemed frightened and explained that a couple of big birds had been chasing him for fun, and so to escape from them he flew up to the top of the tree and saw the nest. He asked if he could hide here until they went away so of course I said he could.

The birds never found him. But as we waited to make sure they had gone away, he told me about his love for singing. He said he sings all the time, whether he is happy, afraid, or sad, and he finds it cheers him up. Can you imagine—a singing bee!

"Anyway, we chatted for a while, then he left and I never saw him again. He was so friendly. In fact he reminded me of you, Deborah. I think he said his name was Burt, or maybe Allen?"

Deborah stared at Kite. She could hardly believe what she was hearing. "Albert? Uncle Albert was here in this nest? Oh, Kite, this is incredible! My uncle went missing a long time ago and we all thought he was... well, you know, and now it's possible that he's alive! It has to be him, he's the only singing bee I know. This is such wonderful news! We have to go find him and bring him home!"

Deborah's wings were beating so fast that she rose up off the nest high above Kite's head.

Kite tried to calm her down. "I'm glad I told you about Albert, and I'm very happy for you, but it's important that you return to your family first. Don't you think they will be worried that something has happened to you? Let's get you home so you can tell your family about your uncle. Then we can come back here and look for him together. I would love to help you find him."

"You're right, Kite. Let's go tell my family the good news. Oh, how incredible to know that Uncle Albert is alive!"

So, after saying goodbye to the eagle king and queen, Deborah and Kite prepared to leave for Bluebell Meadows. Kite was keen to practice his flying skills, and he also wanted to get Deborah safely back home. The young bee climbed up on Kite's back, holding tightly to the feathers between his shoulders.

Kite hesitated just for a moment on the edge of the nest before he launched off and glided away from the tree. He quickly realized how much he loved to fly. He was amazed at how easy it was and how high he could go.

As they flew over the countryside, the two friends talked about everything that had happened the day before. Kite could laugh about his fear of heights now that he was a fully-fledged eagle. His father was right; he was born for this!

Eventually, the land beneath them began to look familiar to Deborah. She inched her way up Kite's feathers to peek over his shoulder for a better view. She searched the meadows below for the old oak tree.

"There's our tree! Look, down there!" she exclaimed. "Our neighbor, Colonel Hoot, lives above us in the same tree. He is the wisest owl in the Ancient Forest and has been a family friend for many years. It's fun to visit him and hear his stories about all the forest animals." She could not wait to see everyone again.

Down, down they flew toward Deborah's tree, landing on a branch close by the entrance to the nest. There was much activity going on as usual with lots of busy bees flying in and out, hard at work. All the activity stopped, of course, when they saw that an eagle had landed in their tree.

Because they were drawing a lot of attention from the worker bees, Deborah and Kite decided to say a quick goodbye before the entire colony came out to investigate.

"Thank you, Kite," she said as she flew down from his shoulder. "This was so much fun!"

"You're welcome," Kite replied. "Perhaps I could come back tomorrow morning and we can go look for Uncle Albert together?"

"Yes, please! I would like that very much. Goodbye, Kite!" she said, as he opened his great wings and soared upwards to the high places beyond the meadows.

Deborah hurried down to the hollow in the tree. She was as happy as a bee could be at the thought of more adventures with Kite. She would see Emeth again and feast on the sunflowers, and she was sure they would find Uncle Albert in no time.

As Deborah entered the bustling nest she suddenly felt very hungry and realized she had not eaten breakfast yet. Honey! That's what she needed, and lots of it. Her wings beat faster at the thought of delicious bluebell honey, drizzled over royal jelly, her most favorite food.

But before she filled her tummy, she needed to find the queen to tell her the exciting news about her uncle. So, darting through the familiar honeycomb maze, she headed straight for her mother's chambers at the center of the colony.

The double doors to the royal throne room were closed when she arrived. Deborah hesitated only for a moment before bursting in to see the queen.

However, as she skidded to a halt in front of the royal throne, the scene before her was not at all what she had expected.

PART 2

Return to Bluebell Meadows

CHAPTER 8
An Unexpected "Welcome"

Deborah looked around the throne room, quite out of breath. She quickly realized that she had burst in on an important gathering and found herself standing in the center of all Queen Miriam's advisors and elders of the colony. Everyone was staring at her, looking very serious indeed.

"Hello, everyone!" she said, attempting a brave smile. No one returned her greeting. The elders were silent. Deborah turned to look at her mother, wondering what was going on.

The queen flew down from her throne and immediately ushered Deborah back through the double doors and out of the royal chambers. The queen heard a low murmuring amongst the elders as she left the room.

Once the doors closed behind them, Queen Miriam turned to face her daughter. "Princess Deborah, where on earth have you been? I have been so worried about you. What happened to you yesterday? Are you hurt? You have a lot of explaining to do!" she said, checking her daughter for injuries.

"Mother, I can explain everything! Really I can, and I will, I promise. I'm fine. I have so much to tell you!" Deborah replied, excited to share her news.

The queen looked troubled.

"Mother, what's going on in there? Why is everyone looking so serious?" Deborah asked. She wondered if something terrible had happened. What other explanation could there be for such a rare gathering of the queen's top advisors?

"Deborah, listen to me. I don't have time to explain now, I have to return to the meeting. Please go to your room and wait for me there. I will come to you as soon as I can, and I will expect a full explanation of your disappearance yesterday. Do not leave your room until I come; do you understand? You are grounded until further notice."

"But Mother, I can explain everything. Please don't ground me! Kite is coming tomorrow and we have to find..." Deborah tried to finish her sentence, but the queen stopped her in mid-flow.

"Deborah, go to your room now—that's an order!" The queen pointed her wing in the direction of her daughter's chamber. The young princess reluctantly obeyed, turning away she flew slowly down the hallway feeling hurt and confused. Queen Miriam went back to the throne room through the double doors which closed behind her.

This was not the "welcome home" she expected at all. What would she tell Kite in the morning when he came to collect her?

CHAPTER 9
Grounded!

Later that morning, the queen knocked gently on Deborah's door and entered. She had calmed down quite a bit and was more like herself, composed, and "queenly."

"Okay, Deborah, I am ready to hear your story, and it had better be a good one."

Her daughter's disappearance yesterday had caused her great concern. But the queen herself had been a lot like Deborah when she was growing up in the nest. She, too, had always been curious about life and full of energy, going off on adventures and leaving her responsibilities. Perhaps Deborah had been eating too much royal jelly lately?

Princess Deborah apologized to her mother for leaving without permission and launched into her tales of adventure at the Big River. She told about meeting Emeth, finding the golden flowers, helping Kite after his fall, escaping the magpie brothers, and spending the night in the royal eagles' nest. Her mother listened patiently while the story poured out of her young daughter.

Deborah saved the news about Uncle Albert until the very end. She explained to her mother how Kite had met Albert in the eagle's nest.

"Kite said he heard singing before Uncle landed right next to him in the nest. Mother, it has to be him! Your brother is alive!" The young princess continued, her wings humming wildly. "And guess what, Mother? Kite's coming here at first light tomorrow to take me back to the Big River so we can go search for him!"

Queen Miriam could hardly believe what she was hearing. She had given up hope of ever knowing what had happened to her long-lost brother. Was there still a chance that she would see him alive again? Her mind was racing as she tried to understand exactly what Deborah was saying.

"Slow down, Deborah, please! This is a lot to take in. So you're telling me that an eagle is coming here in the morning to take you back to the Big River to help you find Albert and bring him home?"

"Yes, Mother!" Deborah said, her hope rising that the queen would allow her to go with Kite. "He will be so happy to meet you. He's very kind and brave. Oh please, Mother, can I go with him, ple-e-e-ase? I promise to be careful and not get into any more trouble with those mean magpies. Kite will be there to protect me, and his father is the king of the skies above the Big River. No one will mess with him!" Deborah was talking faster than ever.

The queen needed a moment to think. It would be hard to say no to her young headstrong daughter whose heart was set on bringing her uncle home safely. But wouldn't it be irresponsible of her to allow her precious daughter, the heir to the royal throne, to face the dangers of such a journey?

She had yet to tell Deborah what had been discussed earlier in the elder's meeting. It was going to be a difficult conversation, but the queen had to do it, and this was the right time.

"Deborah, calm down, please. Before I answer you, there is something important I have to tell you." The young princess sensed this was something serious by the tone of her mother's voice.

"The elders requested a meeting with me this morning to discuss your future. The royal advisors came to me with their concerns about your 'suitability' to be trained as the future queen. They feel your focus is not here with the colony... that you are too 'excitable.' And they are worried that your imagination is 'too wild.'

"Deborah, you are the royal heir to the throne. You will be the queen of this colony one day, and I have to agree that some of their concerns are valid. You don't seem to take your royal calling seriously, and you appear to be more interested in things outside the nest than within it.

"For example, while others are working hard to make honey for the winter months, you spend your time with Colonel Hoot, listening to his stories about the forest animals. Where is your sense of responsibility? Your head is in the clouds! And now you're telling me that your new best friends are an eagle and a butterfly!"

The queen paused for a moment, and tried to calm down. "The elders feel it is time for you to turn your full attention to your royal destiny and the future of this colony. They believe that you should be confined to the nest from now on to learn the responsibilities of being queen."

Deborah was in shock. Time seemed to stand still as the queen's words sank in. Then shock turned to panic at the thought of being trapped indoors every day having "princess lessons". She simply couldn't bear the thought of it.

"Mother, please don't make me do this. I'm not ready for this! I'm not!" She jumped up and began to sob. "I can't, I won't! It's not fair to make me a prisoner here, to never see the meadows again, or visit Colonel Hoot... or go on adventures with Kite! And what about finding Uncle Albert? I have to go find him, Mother—you have to allow it!"

Queen Miriam gathered her thoughts and spoke calmly, "I will decide how we go about finding my brother. It is my responsibility as leader of this colony to make sure Albert is brought home safely. First of all, the royal elders will need to know as soon as possible that he has been seen alive at the Big River. Only then will I make my decision."

Deborah stared at the ground and tried to control her tears. "Please, Mother, if you don't mind, I would like to be alone now." Suddenly Deborah felt overwhelmed, hungry, and exhausted. She needed to sleep for a while.

"Of course, my dear, I understand. You rest now. We can talk more tomorrow." She smiled kindly at the young princess. "Everything will work out, you'll see. I believe in you, Deborah.

You have what it takes to be a great queen."

Deborah forced a weak smile as her mother left the room. As the door closed, she began to sob quietly, crying herself to sleep.

Whatever was she going to do?

CHAPTER 10
Tadpole

Deborah didn't know how long she had been asleep when she heard a soft yet persistent knocking on the door.

"Deborah, it's me. Let me in, let me in!"

She recognized the squeaky voice right away. It was her favorite younger brother, Tadpole. She had nicknamed him Tadpole when he was just a larva forming in the nursery. He had a peculiar shape even then, kind of fat at one end and thin at the other. He reminded her of the tadpoles in the pond she visited each day as she collected water for the colony.

When he had emerged from his cocoon as a baby bee, his head had remained much larger than his body. So the nickname stuck. (His mother, the queen, actually chose the name Theodore for him when he was born, but no one ever called him Theodore.)

"Tadpole! What are you doing here?" asked Deborah as she opened the door to let him in. "To what do I owe the pleasure of having my favorite kid brother come to visit?" Her wings started buzzing loudly. She had a real soft spot for Tadpole. In fact, it was so good to see him that she forgot her sorrows for a moment and gave him a "big sister" kiss on his oversized forehead.

"E-e-w-w-w, stop it! I wish you wouldn't do that, Sis," he said as he squirmed away from her. Both of them were laughing now. He was really glad to see his big sister and secretly loved the attention. Tadpole was very excited and couldn't wait to share his news.

"Hey, Sis, guess what? I know everything about your Big River adventure yesterday. I can't wait to meet your friend Kite tomorrow and see a real eagle close up! Sis, you have to introduce me to him!"

Deborah's eyes got wide. "Wait... WHAT!? How do you know about Kite? What do you mean you know everything? How?" His sister was horrified that he knew the details of her story already.

"It's okay, it's okay, only me and Honeysuckle know, and we swore each other to secrecy. What happened was, we were playing hide and seek with cousin Buzby earlier, and it was Buzby's turn to find us, so me and Honeysuckle went to look for a good place to hide.

"I had the brilliant idea to go to Aunt Primrose's chamber. You know how her room is full of all that stuff she's collected over the years?

Anyway, we had just found the perfect hiding place behind a stack of old honey pots, when we heard voices and Mother and Aunt Primrose came  in! Mother was talking really, really fast and her wings were buzzing like crazy, like yours do when you're excited. We didn't know what to do so we kept really quiet and got to hear everything they were talking about. Mother was telling Aunt Primrose about the cool butterfly you met, the golden flowers, meeting Kite, and all the cool stuff you did. Wow, Sis, that is one serious adventure! I wish I could have been there with you!"

Her brother was so excited, he was buzzing all over the room like a mini tornado as he went on, "Then Mother told her that Uncle Albert is alive! Wowee! You found the golden flowers, met an eagle, and discovered that our uncle isn't dead—all in one day!"

His big face was glowing with awe and wonder at his older sibling. She had become his number one hero overnight.

Deborah ignored her brother's compliment, "Hang on, slow down, slow down. What exactly did Mother say about Uncle Albert?"

"She told her how Uncle had met Kite in the eagles' nest. Then Mother asked Auntie if she should allow you and Kite to go find Uncle Albert tomorrow, or if she should send out a search party to go to the Big River to look for him. She's arranged a big meeting of the elders tonight to tell them everything and make a plan. Oh, Sis, I wish I could go with the search party but they'd say I was too young. They would never let me go." Tadpole looked sad and disappointed at the thought of missing out on such a great adventure.

Deborah tried to keep her brother focused on the important details. "Well? So what did Aunt Primrose say? Tell me!"

"Auntie told Mother to go visit the Colonel and ask his advice. Colonel Hoot will know what to do. That's what you always say, right Sis?"

Deborah leapt up, thinking fast. She had slept through the afternoon, and the meeting with the elders was probably about to begin.

"Tadpole, I have to know what happens. Kite will be here early tomorrow morning. There's no time to waste, let's go to that meeting!"

CHAPTER 11
Colonel Hoot

Meanwhile, after talking with Primrose, Queen Miriam slipped out of the nest unnoticed to pay a visit to the Colonel. Her wise old friend lived in the heart of the tree above their nest. She needed his advice. He was the only one she knew who could help her make the right decision for everyone concerned.

Colonel Hoot had been their neighbor for as long as she could remember. He had also been her mother's faithful advisor before the queen was even born. The Colonel was the one the royal family relied on when difficult decisions had to be made for the good of the colony, decisions that needed a special kind of wisdom. The old owl had proved to be a great friend on many occasions.

Although the queen disapproved of Deborah leaving her duties to spend time with the Colonel, she was secretly pleased that her daughter was forming her own friendship with the wise bird. Princess Deborah would need his counsel in the years ahead when she finally became queen of the colony.

It was late afternoon as the queen flew up to the entrance of the hollow in the great tree. She knew that Colonel Hoot would be waking up from his nap as the sun was setting.

She called out into the caverns of the old tree, "Colonel, are you there? It's me, Miriam. I need to speak with you. Hello, are you there?"

The owl's booming voice echoed from deep inside, "Hello-o-o-o, Miriam! How good it is to hear your voice! Please come i-i-n-n-n, come i-i-n-n-n!"

The queen had visited the Colonel's home many times before. Once her eyes adjusted to the darkness inside the tree, she made her way past the entrance where a soft light shone in from the setting sun.

As usual, the Colonel was perched in the middle of the room, surrounded by his collection of old books and maps of the forest. He was an avid reader, and part of his evening routine was to read about the many animals who made the Ancient Forest their home.

Queen Miriam felt comfortable here among the Colonel's well-used books which covered the floor. She loved everything about this old room and how it always smelled "green," like a mixture of fresh leaves, moss, and wood. In this familiar place she began to relax.

"Dear Colonel, how are you this evening? It's been a while since I have seen you. Are you well?"

The old owl seemed to fill the room. His brown-and-black feathers were ruffled to keep him warm in the cool of the late afternoon. He was delighted to see his friend of many years.

"I am very well thank you, my dear. I was studying my forest animal books just now, learning more about the beaver. Cousin Barnaby reported a sighting of this animal a few nights ago far out on the west side. He described it as a huge rodent, brown in color, with a thick, shaggy coat, stubby legs, and a tail like a paddle. Have you ever heard of a beaver in the Ancient Forest, Miriam?"

"Er, no I'm afraid I have not. But it does sound very interesting indeed." The queen was used to the Colonel's random facts and questions having known him for so long.

"Oh, please forgive me, dear Miriam. I am sure you didn't come here to listen to me rambling on about beavers!" He lifted his head back and laughed his deep owl laugh, "Hoooo, hoooo, hooo!" He blinked his big, round eyes twice and fixed them on the queen. His tufted ears faced her and she knew she had his full attention.

"Now, my dear, how are you and the family? Is there anything I can help you with? How is Princess Deborah today?"

"Well, that's what I'm here to speak with you about: the young princess. Generally she's doing well, thank you. Healthy and headstrong as always." She smiled as she thought of her daughter. "I value your advice, Colonel. I have a difficult decision to make tonight, and I would greatly appreciate your wisdom." The old owl nodded, encouraging her to share her burden with him as she had done many times before.

So the queen told him how the young princess had disappeared yesterday without telling anyone, returning this morning full of stories of her adventures at the Big River. She gave him a brief overview of all Deborah had shared with her, ending with the incredible news that her brother had been seen alive. The queen explained that she had summoned the elders together this very evening to inform them about Albert and to discuss a plan of action to rescue her brother.

"Deborah wants my permission to go back to the Big River to find Albert with her eagle friend, Kite. She has already arranged for Kite to come to the nest in the morning and take her back there. So this is my dilemma: can I allow Deborah to go back to the Big River on such a dangerous mission to find Albert? I mean, wouldn't it be irresponsible of me to do so as her mother and leader?"

The queen was feeling the burden of having to make the right decision for her daughter, as well as for her brother and the rest of the colony.

She continued, "I realize that Kite knows the Big River. He grew up there, and his family has lived there for many generations. Sending Deborah and Kite would make more sense than sending a search party of elders who have never ventured further than this meadow. None of my advisors have ever experienced the outside world or the dangers they might encounter.

"Also, if a search party of bees shows up in another colony's territory, they would only draw attention to themselves. No one would notice Deborah as a single bee, and she would have Kite's protection. Plus they would have the help of Kite's parents, the eagle king and queen. What do you think I should do, Colonel?" She looked to her friend, waiting for his wise counsel.

The great owl understood the queen had a difficult decision to make, and he was quiet for a moment, thinking carefully before he spoke. His eyes blinked several times as he pondered all the facts.

"Dear Miriam, listen to your heart. What is your heart telling you to do? You know your daughter better than anyone else. Do you feel that Deborah is ready to be sent out to find her uncle with this young eagle?"

She thought for a moment before she gave her answer. "In my heart of hearts, I believe she is."

There was silence in the hollow of the tree. The Colonel's ears twitched. He could sense the inner battle the queen was having as she tried to fully embrace what she believed. She was torn as a mother, even though she knew her daughter had the ability and courage to succeed.

"Trust yourself, Miriam. You are an excellent leader, and you have given your life to serve the colony. Every bee knows you have their best interests at heart, and so does your daughter. They will accept your final decision. Could it be that Deborah needs your trust in her to do this, to learn to trust herself and to develop her leadership skills? Your decision to let her go could be the making of her as a courageous leader and future queen of the colony.

"You came here tonight for my advice, so here it is: go to the meeting and tell the elders about Albert. Let them ask questions so they fully understand the situation. Make sure they know there will be many dangers to face. Keep the focus on finding Albert, not about Deborah and her disappearance yesterday. Then, ask the elders if any among them would be willing to go to the Big River and lead the search for your brother. If no one steps forward, then you will have your answer."

Queen Miriam returned to the nest that evening with the Colonel's wise words playing over in her mind. Now she knew what she must do.

CHAPTER 12
The Final Decision

Tadpole and Deborah flew through the long, familiar hallways to the royal chambers in the heart of the colony where the queen had summoned all the elders together. They knew they would never be allowed to attend such an important gathering, and Deborah was supposed to be grounded in her room. But they had a secret hiding place in the wall behind the royal throne room. It was a long-abandoned storeroom that Tadpole and his cousins had once discovered while playing hide and seek.

Tadpole got there first. He tucked his wings in close to his body and squeezed through the secret doorway. Deborah followed him inside. They could see most of what was happening in the throne room through a hole in the wall, and took turns peeking through to see who was speaking.

The queen was addressing the elders now, saying, "Elders of the colony, I have called this meeting tonight because some important news, very 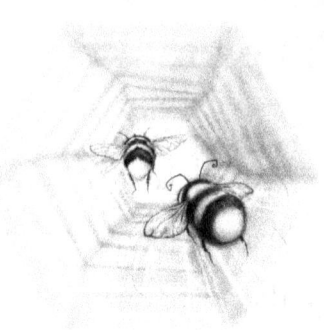 good news, has come to my attention concerning my brother, Albert." All eyes were fixed on their leader as she continued, "My daughter, Princess Deborah, was informed by a reliable source that Albert has been seen at the Big River. I am thrilled to announce that my brother is alive!" The whole room gasped at the news, and the sound of humming bee wings became louder as the excitement grew.

The queen raised her voice above the noise, "Quiet please, everyone! Quiet, please! There is much to discuss tonight. We need to make a plan of action and decide how we are going to find our beloved Albert and bring him home. Now, I'm sure you have many questions. I am happy to try and answer them as best I can. Please, let's keep our focus on finding Albert and bringing him safely back to the colony."

Several elders asked about exactly when and where he had been seen, and where the queen thought Albert was now. She answered as honestly as she could with the few facts she had been given by Deborah.

"I have a question, Your Highness." Everyone turned to look at the old bee at the back of the room close to where Deborah and her brother were hiding.

Elder Cranberry was one of the oldest and grumpiest bees in the colony. He was well known for having a short temper and being hard to please. He had very little patience with the younger bees, and had no time for Princess Deborah and her "stories".

"My queen, please can you tell us more about this 'reliable source' you mentioned? I am sure we are all curious to know where this information came from." He looked around the room and everyone nodded in agreement. They turned to look at Queen Miriam.

She paused for a moment before she answered, "The reliable source of which I speak, according to my daughter, is a young eagle named Kite, who Deborah met yesterday at the Big River. Apparently Kite had a short visit from Albert in the eagles' nest not too long ago. They talked for a while and then he left. Kite reported to Deborah that Albert seemed to be in good health."

Elder Cranberry could not contain himself, "Bah! I knew it! That willful young bee left her duties at the nest yesterday, flew to the Big River alone, and told no one of her whereabouts. She's completely irresponsible, that's what she is!"

There was a low murmuring among the elders, followed by an uncomfortable silence.

Queen Miriam had been expecting something like this from Elder Cranberry, who had always questioned Deborah's suitability to becoming queen one day. Her voice was stern but calm as she responded to his unkind outburst, "Elder Cranberry, I would like to remind you that Princess Deborah is my daughter and heir to this throne. I respectfully ask that you keep your opinions about her behavior to yourself. This meeting is in session only to discuss how we can successfully rescue Albert and return him to the safety of the colony."

The queen managed to keep her royal composure.

Tadpole and Deborah looked at each other in their secret hideout. They were impressed by the way their mother handled the difficult old bee. This was turning out to be a very interesting meeting indeed!

The queen continued, "Are there any more questions?" She looked around the room, but no one spoke up. "Very well then," she went on, "We will now discuss how to go about finding Albert and bringing him back to the colony. First of all, is there anyone here tonight who is willing to lead the search party to the Big River and find Albert? This will be a dangerous mission—there is no doubt about that. We do not know where he is, neither do we know anything about the land around the Big River or who lives there. The search could take many days. Now, is anyone here willing to go?"

There was a long, awkward silence in the room. Deborah and Tadpole held their breath. Nobody spoke. Only the sound of shifting bodies and rustling wings could be heard. The elders were feeling uncomfortable, many of them looking down, avoiding eye contact with their leader.

The queen looked slowly back and forth across the room.

"I see. Well then, you have left me no choice. This is my decision based on your response: I will be sending my daughter, Princess Deborah, to the Big River tomorrow with Kite to find Albert. Kite will be here first thing in the morning. I will inform my daughter of the decision that has been made. That is all. This meeting is now officially closed."

Deborah was overjoyed! Her mother was actually sending her out on the rescue mission with

Kite! She was going back to the Big River after all.

She grabbed hold of Tadpole and squeezed him tight in her excitement, exclaiming, "Wow! I can hardly believe it! I'm going with Kite tomorrow to search for Uncle Albert! Come on, Tad, let's get out of here before anyone sees us!"

The meeting was over, and the elders would soon be leaving the royal chamber. Before they could get caught, the siblings left their hiding place and raced back to their rooms for the evening.

Deborah's heart was pounding as she closed her door that night. She did not even try to sleep. She lay on her bed wide awake and waited for the morning to come. Uncle Albert was out there somewhere, and with Kite's help, she was determined to find him and bring him home.

CHAPTER 13
Permission Granted!

The queen did not sleep a wink that night. As she lay down in her chambers, she felt the weight of royal responsibility from her decision. Deborah was young and inexperienced, and there were many dangers beyond Bluebell Meadows. Still, the queen sensed that the young princess was ready. She felt she had made the right decision, in spite of how her mother's heart was feeling.

This assignment to rescue Albert was an important part of Deborah's training as the future queen of the colony. It would demand courage in action, something that every great leader needed to find within themselves.

At first light the next morning, Queen Miriam knocked gently and entered her daughter's chamber. She was unaware that the young princess already knew of the queen's decision the night before.

"Good morning, my dear. I trust you had a restful night."

Deborah replied as calmly as she could, "Good morning, Mother." The young bee felt like she might burst with excitement at any moment.

"Deborah, I have something important to tell you. I called a meeting of the elders last night while you were sleeping, and told them the good news about your uncle. As you can imagine, everyone was thrilled to hear that he is alive and well. After a great deal of thought, I want to let you know who I am sending to the Big River to find Albert."

Deborah didn't trust herself to speak. All she could manage to do was nod her head rapidly as her mother kept talking.

"I have thought long and hard about this and have decided that you, my dear daughter, are the one I am sending to find your unc–"

Before the queen could finish saying the word "uncle," Deborah lunged forward and wrapped her wings around her mother, squealing with delight.

"Mother, thank you! Thank you so-o-o much! I won't let you down. We will find Uncle Albert and bring him home. Oh, I can't wait to tell Kite when he gets here! Thank you! Thank you for trusting me. You won't regret this—I promise!"

Deborah released her mother and began flying around her room in circles. The queen loved seeing Deborah so happy even if her daughter's excitement was making her dizzy. Queen Miriam knew she had made the right decision.

Just then, the celebration was interrupted by a loud knocking on Deborah's door. Her mother opened it to find one of her senior advisors looking disturbed and shaken.

"My queen, your presence is requested outside the nest at once. A huge eagle has landed in our tree and it's asking for Princess Deborah!"

"Kite is here! He's here!" Deborah shouted joyfully, "Mother, please come and meet him."

"Yes, yes, I'm coming. You go ahead, I'll be there in a moment," she replied.

Deborah squeezed past the queen and her nervous advisor, hurrying as fast as she could to go meet Kite. Queen Miriam shook her head and gathered her composure. This was a big moment for her as a mother to see her daughter, heir to the throne, leave the nest with an eagle the queen had never even met. She could already feel the emotion welling up.

Taking a deep breath, she followed her daughter. She was about to meet a real eagle.

PART 3
The Rescue

CHAPTER 14

Let the Journey Begin!

Kite's arrival at the nest that morning was causing quite a stir. When the colony heard that an eagle had landed in their tree, every single bee made its way to the entrance to take a look.

Tadpole was one of the first on the scene. Not everyone knew what he already knew about this giant bird and the rescue mission to the Big River. He grinned as he overheard some of the conversations going on around him.

"What's it doing here? Is it going to eat us?" asked one. "Do eagles eat bees? Colonel Hoot would know."

"I've never seen an eagle up close. It's ginormous!" said another.

"I wish somebody would tell us what's going on!" another remarked.

The humming of small bee wings became louder and louder as the excitement grew. Tadpole looked for Deborah among the crowd forming at a safe distance around Kite. He pushed his way to the front just in time to see his sister flying out of the nest at top speed to meet the feathered visitor. This was his moment. Tadpole darted up to join Deborah as she arrived to greet Kite. The crowd watched in awe.

Deborah was clearly delighted to see her new friend again. She was talking very fast, her wings humming wildly as she twirled and danced in mid-air around the young eagle's head. The princess seemed to have forgotten everyone else around her, including her brother who was desperate for an introduction.

As soon as she paused to draw a breath, Tadpole jumped into the conversation, "Hello, Kite! I'm Tadpole, Deborah's favorite kid brother. Hey, is it true that eagles eat bees and slugs? Do you live in a pile of sticks? Do you have any brothers and sisters?" Tadpole was thrilled to meet a real eagle and all his questions poured out at once.

Kite's laugh was friendly and genuine as he replied, "Ah, Tadpole, it is very good to meet you! I can see you are just as curious as your big sister. No, you can rest assured we don't eat bees or slugs, and yes I do live in a nest of sticks high up in the tallest tree at the Big River. Our family has lived there for many generations. And no, I don't have any brothers and sisters."

"Tadpole, stop grilling Kite with your silly questions!" Deborah said, laughing at her younger brother who was feeling more confident now. Tadpole was buzzing all around the big bird, in awe of his sharp talons and curved beak.

Deborah continued, "Mother will be here soon. You've said hello, now off you go. I'll see you when we get back, okay?" As she was encouraging Tadpole to leave, the queen arrived. Deborah was excited to introduce Kite to her mother.

The young eagle bowed his head as Queen Miriam joined her daughter. "Your Majesty, it is a great honor to meet you," he said humbly.

"And it's a pleasure to meet you, Kite. Deborah has told me all about you and how you protected her at the Big River. I want to thank you for your kindness." Although the queen didn't show it, she too was in awe of this giant bird. He was very impressive!

The queen continued, "Now, I want you to know that I have confidence in you both to find

Uncle Albert and bring him home. You have my blessing and my full support. Please remember, however, that there will be dangers along the way, so be alert and stay together at all times. Kite, I speak for the elders as well as the entire colony when I say how grateful we are that you will be beside Princess Deborah as her protector."

Kite assured the queen, "Your Majesty, thank you for trusting me with the safety of your daughter. I will not let you down."

Queen Miriam was comforted by his words. "Now, you have a long journey ahead of you, so don't delay. I will look forward to your safe return to the nest."

The queen suddenly felt overwhelmed with emotion. It was hard to watch her brave young daughter leaving the safety of the colony. She quickly turned away and returned to the privacy of her chamber where she could be alone. She did not want Deborah to see her tears.

After her mother left, the young princess said to Kite, "Okay, my friend, let's go!"

And to the crowd around them she called out, "Goodbye, everyone!"

She took her position on Kite's back. As he launched off the branch, Kite let out a loud screech that echoed throughout the valley, his huge wings slowly beating the air. Up they went, higher and higher, far above the tree line in the direction of the Big River. The journey had begun!

What the two friends didn't know was that they were not alone...

CHAPTER 15
The Stowaway

Tadpole held on tight as Kite's huge body lifted up off the branch and climbed into the sky. Each flap of the eagle's strong wings took them higher and higher. The young bee had never been so far above the ground in all his life! This was going to be so much fun!

He giggled as he thought about the look he'd see on his sister's face when they arrived at the Big River and she found out that he had stowed away in Kite's feathers. While the queen had been talking with Kite and Deborah, Tadpole had carefully hidden underneath the eagle's tail. Then he quickly shuffled into position right before take-off and held on for dear life.

What a ride! They flew for a very long time over meadows, streams, and herds of grazing cows. As they cruised high in the sky, Deborah and Kite discussed their mission to find her missing uncle.

"Kite, where should we start our search?" she asked. "We know that Uncle Albert is alive and living somewhere at the Big River but we don't have much to go on."

"You're right, your uncle could be anywhere. So last night I asked my parents if they had any suggestions for where we might look, and my father had a great idea. He told me about an old friend of his, an ancient trout who lives upstream from the sunflower meadows in the Quiet Pool. His name is Admiral Salmo Trutt. He's famous on the river for outsmarting many otters and herons over the years and living to a great old age. The Admiral knows everyone and everything that happens in and around the Big River. My father thinks it's possible he could know something about your uncle."

The eagle king had given his son some wise advice about Admiral Trutt, knowing that the old fish could be grumpy and difficult at times, especially if woken from one of his naps. The king gave Kite the secret to having a successful visit with the Admiral—mayflies! Salmo Trutt could not resist a snack of mayflies; they were his favorite food. The eagle king advised his son to approach the pool with a mouthful of mayflies as a friendship offering, just in case he woke up in a bad mood.

Kite continued, "Papa said he won't be grumpy for long once he sees the mayfly snack, and will tell me anything I want to know."

They both laughed at the thought of bringing mayflies to a bad-tempered old trout, but at least it gave them a good place to start.

Deborah agreed with the plan and replied, "Alright then, we will begin our search with a visit to

Admiral Salmo Trutt!"

Kite soared high above the land for many miles until the Big River finally came into view. As the young princess looked down at the river below she realized how much she felt at home here. It was a place of great beauty and abundance. Deborah could not wait to see her new friend Emeth and feast on the sunflowers once again.

From his hiding place in Kite's feathers, Tadpole was in awe to see the Big River for the first time. He could hardly believe his eyes. If only cousin Buzby and Honeysuckle could see him now!

Kite headed down toward the familiar meadow by the still waters where the sheep were grazing and the golden flowers were swaying in the breeze.

Deborah felt hungry and decided to eat breakfast first. After all, no important mission should start on an empty stomach. Down they went to  the pasture at the river's edge where Kite landed on a large grassy mound. Deborah flew up from Kite's back and was just about to congratulate him on a great landing when she heard a strange noise.

"Aaarrrgghh!"

"What was that?" Deborah asked, looking at her friend curiously. The sound was coming from Kite!

Before Kite had time to reply, the stowaway tumbled out from the eagle's feathers and rolled across the grass in front of them, head over wings.

Deborah could not believe her eyes!

"TADPOLE!" They stared in disbelief at the pear-shaped little bee who was picking himself up off the ground.

"Wowee, that was one scary landing!" said Tadpole, wide-eyed as he shook himself and stretched out his crumpled wings.

"OH NO! NO NO!" cried Deborah, "What do you think you are doing here, Tadpole? This is no place for you! What on earth are you thinking?" Deborah was furious.

"I am thinking...how awesome these flowers are!" Tadpole said, looking around in amazement, ignoring his sister's questions. "Wow, so these are the golden flowers we've been hearing about forever! Cool! I'm so-o-o hungry!" And with that, he flew up and plunged headfirst into the nearest sunflower.

"Oh no you don't!" said Deborah, "Come back here this minute! Mother will be frantic with worry when she realizes you're missing." Tadpole didn't seem to hear her, so she flew up to join him, trying to resist diving into the sweet nectar herself. She spoke firmly to her brother, "You can't do this, Tad. This won't work. You being here will only hold us back."

She turned to Kite. "Kite, help me. Please make him understand this won't work!" She looked with pleading eyes at her friend who was trying his best to look serious. Kite's eyes twinkled with amusement as he replied,

"Seems to me like young Tadpole has made up his mind. He kind of reminds me of someone else I know."

Deborah was mad with her little brother, but what could she do? Tadpole was here, and it would take far too long to return him to Bluebell Meadows now. But even though she was angry with him she understood why he wanted to come. This could be his one and only chance to see the Big River and have a real adventure away from the colony. Deborah sighed a deep sigh.

"Okay, okay." She turned to her brother whose head was still buried inside the flower, "You can stay, but you have to listen to us and do exactly what Kite and I tell you to do. You can't go off on your own, ever. You must stay with us at all times. Do you understand?"

Tadpole's head popped up, covered in pollen. "Yes, Sis, I'll be good, I promise. I won't leave your side. I'll help you find Uncle Albert. You'll be glad I came, you'll see."

Tadpole couldn't be happier as he filled his honey-tummy that morning. This was by far the best day of his life.

Shaking her head, Deborah tucked into the feast next to him. Kite took a long drink from the river, chuckling to himself. It would be fun having Tadpole around. He was becoming fond of the young bee already.

Kite was sure of one thing—he would need to be extra watchful now that he had two lives to protect as they began the search for Uncle Albert.

CHAPTER 16
The Song of the Sunflowers

While Deborah and Tadpole were happily feeding on the sunflowers, Kite decided to go upstream to visit the old trout at his home in the Quiet Pool. He wanted to find out if this ancient fish had any information for them about the missing bee. And so, following the directions to the pool his father had given him, he set off in search of Admiral Trutt.

Meanwhile, Tadpole was overjoyed to be at the Big River, just like his sister had been the day she arrived with Emeth. All he wanted to do was eat, explore, and eat some more! Deborah decided it was safe to let him go off on his own for a short time, as long as he came back as soon as Kite returned.

"But you must stay where I can see you!" she called after him, as he darted off to explore the moment she gave him permission.

Deborah settled into the petals of a large sunflower, feeling full and content. It was quiet and peaceful in the meadows. The birds were chirping and chattering with one another as the river moved calmly by. This was the perfect time to rest before Kite returned from the Quiet Pool.

As Deborah relaxed into the soft petals, she started to daydream. She was not thinking of anything in particular when suddenly she began to feel a strong desire to sing. It was the same strong urge she had felt the first time she visited the sunflowers with Emeth. Only this time, the passion inside her was even more powerful. It took her by surprise, and she felt like she would burst if she didn't let it out!

Deborah scanned the meadow for Tadpole and saw him a short distance away, his head buried deep inside a golden flower. She could not ignore this strong desire any longer. Taking a deep breath, she simply allowed it to bubble up. Then the strangest thing began to happen: a song rose up from within her, flooding her with a melody that she had never heard before but was somehow familiar to her.

What was even more surprising was that when she opened her mouth to let the song out, the sunflowers around her began to join in! Their sound was the most beautiful chorus she had ever heard—it was heavenly! It was as if this song had been sleeping within her. Deborah sensed at that moment that the sunflowers had been waiting for her to sing it with them:

Come join with nature's chorus, sing!
Sing aloud, from deep within!
Awake your sound and enter in,
Oh sing the song of ages!

Sing with sunflowers, birds and trees,
Revive the ancient song of bees!
We long to hear your freedom song,
Come, sing the song of ages!

This poem of nature freely sing
Let your song bring joy within
Awake, awake, let's all join in
The joyful song of ages!

Then the song simply faded. Deborah lay very still, trying to take in what had just happened. How was it possible that she was able to sing a song that she had never heard before? What did it mean to *revive the ancient song of bees*? She didn't understand it, but she sensed that something had been awakened within her. She felt freer somehow.

Just as she was pondering this new and wonderful experience with the flowers, she heard a beautiful, clear voice calling out from the sky somewhere above her head.

"Deborah, Deborah! It's you! I knew you'd come!" It was Emeth!

That same morning, the heavenly butterfly had been feasting at the red poppy fields far away when all of a sudden she knew she must go to the Big River at once. She followed her instincts and was delighted to see Deborah resting on the sunflower.

"Emeth! How wonderful to see you again!" Deborah said as she flew up to greet her in the air. "I was hoping we would see you today. I have so much to tell you!"

The sunflowers seemed happy that the two friends were reunited, as they nodded their golden heads in the breeze. Deborah decided not to tell her friend about singing with the flowers. She couldn't explain it even if she tried. Instead, she shared with Emeth all that had happened since they last met.

As Deborah finished telling Emeth about the rescue mission to find Uncle Albert and bring him home, Tadpole arrived covered in pollen. Deborah introduced him to Emeth.

The butterfly was delighted to meet Tadpole. Emeth was completely unaware that he had invited himself to the Big River as a stowaway and said to him kindly, "Tadpole, how wonderful that you chose to join your sister and support her on this important rescue mission. Your sister is a brave adventurer with a courageous heart, and I see that you are following the same path." Her colorful wings were dazzling in the sunlight. Tadpole beamed with delight. He had never met a more lovely creature—so kind and beautiful. The young bee began to feel like he was meant to be here at the Big River. His sister was also starting to feel better about having her kid brother around. After all, he had decided to come along fully aware of the possible dangers, and that meant a lot to her.

Emeth continued, "Deborah, I'm so glad to hear your uncle has been seen alive. I know many of the creatures who call the Big River their home. I can ask around if anyone has seen him recently if you would like. I would love to help you find him."

Deborah immediately agreed. She was pleased that Emeth would be joining the search for her uncle.

Just then, Kite returned from his visit upstream, landing on a rock in the shallows that was much too small for his large body. He didn't seem to mind; he just spread his wings wide as he swayed in the breeze to keep his balance.

Kite was delighted to see Emeth had found Deborah and Tadpole. "Emeth! What a pleasure to see you again. Welcome to the search and rescue party!"

The young eagle couldn't wait to tell them all about his visit with Admiral Trutt. "Deborah, I have great news! I found the old trout sound asleep in the pool underneath the rock just as my father had described. The mayfly snack worked perfectly. The Admiral was in a good mood and was more than happy to talk to me. He wants to meet you in person! He said he has information for you about your uncle." Kite seemed very pleased with himself.

"That is wonderful news, Kite! Now we have a place to start our search." Deborah was feeling encouraged. "Come on everyone, it's time to meet the Admiral and find out what he knows about Uncle Albert."

So the small party of friends left the sunflower meadows and followed Kite upstream to meet Admiral Salmo Trutt.

CHAPTER 17
The Pike

It was a beautiful summer's day as the rescue party set out together flying low over the water, following the bends and curves of the Big River.

Kite led the way, followed by Emeth and Tadpole. Deborah followed behind, happily watching her little brother and Emeth getting to know one another. She was thankful for each of these wonderful companions who had joined her in the search for Uncle Albert.

All of a sudden, Deborah saw a glint of silver in the water ahead. Perhaps it was just the sun reflecting on the surface? But no—there it was again! And this time she saw a dark shape moving beneath Tadpole and Emeth.

Deborah did not have time to warn them. Before she could call out, she watched with horror as a long silver fish burst out of the river with its mouth wide open and plucked Tadpole from the air. By the time she shouted, "Noo-o-o-o!" the fish had already returned to the water with a great splash!

She darted forward as fast as she could to Emeth, who was hovering above the surface where the fish had disappeared. Both friends tried frantically to see beneath the water for any sign of Tadpole or the silver pike who snatched him.

"Kite, Kite, come quickly!" Deborah cried, "Tadpole's been swallowed by a fish!" Immediately, Kite swung around and joined the others who were helplessly flying in circles.

"We've lost him! It happened so fast. Kite, what are we going to do?" Deborah was beside herself at the thought of losing her little brother.

Kite wasted no time. He told Deborah and Emeth to move to safety at the edge of the river. He flew up high above them and circled around, searching for any sign of movement in the waters below. Then suddenly, Kite folded back his wings as his eyes locked on to his target in the river. Like an arrow from the sky, the young eagle plunged down and entered the water feet first with a mighty splash!

Deborah and Emeth gasped as Kite's whole body went under the water. As they watched from the riverbank everything seemed to happen in slow motion. All they could see were brown feathers thrashing and splashing. Then the surface of the river became strangely still.

"Come on!" said Deborah. The two friends raced over to where Kite had plunged in. They called out his name over and over, flying around in circles. Time went by slowly as they waited anxiously, looking for signs of life in the deep water. Had Kite drowned trying to save Tadpole?

All of a sudden the river erupted around them as Kite's wet, feathered head appeared, followed by his drenched body, then wings, and finally feet which were holding on to a large silver pike. Kite had caught the fish that swallowed Tadpole!

Keeping a tight hold on the wriggling creature, Kite flew above the water with his prize to a flat rock at the side of the river. Deborah and Emeth rushed over to join him.

Kite was panting from his efforts underwater, his wet feathers sticking out in all directions. He looked down at the scaly thief who was gulping the air.

Kite gripped the pike in his talons. "I don't know who you are, but you had better release that bee right now!" he ordered. "Give us our friend back or you will never see this river again!"

"Okay, okay, you're hurting me. I'll let the insect go when you let go of me," gurgled the helpless fish, looking up at his attacker.

"I will let you go when you release the bee and not before!" replied Kite as he squeezed a little harder to make his point.

The pike could see he was in no position to argue, so he reluctantly opened his mouth. With a cough and a splutter, Tadpole bounced onto the rock next to Kite. Deborah was at her brother's side in a flash.

"Tad, Tad, are you okay? Wake up, wake up! Speak to me, Tad!" She darted around his limp body looking for any sign of life from the bedraggled bee.

At last, Tadpole blinked several times and gulped some fresh air. He looked up at his sister.

"Whoa, Sis, that was crazy! Everything went dark and spooky. And there was a really bad smell of fish. What just happened?"

Deborah and Emeth were so relieved they burst out laughing. Tadpole was unharmed. The young bee smelled fishy, but no one seemed to mind. His friends were overjoyed to have him back on dry land.

"Kite dived into the river to save you. Look! He's still holding the fish who snatched you."

Tadpole could not believe his eyes when he saw the silver pike wriggling in Kite's talons. He got up, shook himself, and went to take a better look, keeping well clear of the pike's open mouth.

"Wowee! Kite, you dived into the river to save me?" asked the young bee as he tried to take it all in. "Rescued from the belly of a fish by an eagle! My friends back home will never believe this!"

Kite was still dripping wet and shook himself, giving everyone a cool shower. "It seems I have a gift for rescuing bees!" he said with a twinkle in his eye, making everyone laugh. Everyone except the pike that is. The fish was still firmly in the eagle's talons, but Kite kept his word and released his grip. The scaly predator flopped back into the river and swam away.

Deborah joined Tadpole at Kite's side, breathing a sigh of relief. "Kite, how can we ever thank you? You knew exactly what to do and didn't hesitate to do it!"

Emeth agreed, "Kite, you saved Tadpole's life. That was a very brave rescue. I have never seen anything like that before. Well done!"

The four friends stayed huddled together on the big rock, realizing how close they had come to losing young Tadpole that day.

"From now on let's make sure we fly much higher above the water, well beyond the reach of hungry fish. Agreed?" said Deborah, and everyone agreed.

Her mother was right; this was a dangerous mission and they needed to stay alert, be watchful, and keep close to Kite.

CHAPTER 18
Admiral Salmo Trutt

Admiral Trutt was stirring from his lunchtime nap in the Quiet Pool. Earlier that morning he had been woken from a deep sleep by an unexpected visitor. It was a young eagle, the son of his old friend the eagle king. The large brown bird had brought a tasty treat of mayflies and wanted information about a missing honey bee named Albert.

The Admiral had great respect for the eagle king and queen. Their friendship went back many years, so because of that—and the mayflies, of course—he was willing to share what he knew.

The ancient fish might be too old to get through the day without several naps, but he knew exactly who was doing what, when, and where on the river.

In fact, the missing bee had appeared on the rock above the Admiral's pool just a few days earlier, and not for the first time. This bee had the annoying habit of singing loudly at the top of its voice when the old trout was trying to sleep. Salmo Trutt was getting tired of being disturbed by this crazy singing bee. It was unacceptable behavior, and something had to be done.

So when Albert showed up a few days ago waking Salmo Trutt from his sleep yet again with loud singing, it was the last straw. The trout swam up to the surface of the pool and thrashed his tail in the water to get the bee's attention.

"Excuse me, you up there!" he shouted. "Do you mind? I'm trying to get some sleep down here! I cannot hear myself think with you making all that noise. What's your name, old boy, and why do you keep coming here?"

Albert looked down into the water to see who was doing all the splashing.

"Hello there!" said the friendly old bee, peering over the edge of the rock. He didn't seem to have heard anything the Admiral said, probably because of the loud splashing.

The trout called up, "Look, old boy, the name's Admiral Trutt. I would greatly appreciate it if you would buzz off and find another place to do your singing. I've lived in this river for a long time. This is my pool and my rock, and I like it quiet around here."

The Admiral stared up at Albert with unblinking, unfriendly eyes and waited for him to leave. The annoying bee got the message and left, and the old trout swam back down to his resting place beneath the rock. Thankfully, that was the last time he saw the singing bee.

After Tadpole and Kite had dried off, the four friends continued their journey to the Quiet Pool. They decided it would be a lot safer if they all traveled on Kite's back after what had happened with the pike. Tadpole could not have been happier!

The young bee asked if he could ride on top of Kite's head so he could see everything Kite could see. The eagle was like a superhero to Tadpole. His cousins would be so jealous if they could see him now. He talked non-stop to Kite as they flew along the river, asking him a hundred and one questions about his life growing up in the eagles' nest. Tadpole was having the time of his life!

Emeth and Deborah were content to lie back and relax, resting between Kite's shoulders. They were an unusual sight as they flew upstream together that day.

Kite gathered a mouthful of mayflies along the way to take as an offering to the Admiral.

It was mid-afternoon when the four friends finally arrived at the bend in the river where the old trout lived.

Kite landed quietly on the flat rock above the Admiral's pool. He peered over the edge and saw the dark shape of the fish's body lying still in the water below. Kite's shadow fell across the surface of the pool as he leaned over to drop the mayflies into the water. The Admiral knew immediately that he had visitors. He'd been expecting them. It was as if Admiral Trutt had a sixth sense.

"Ah there you are, young prince," he gurgled as his head popped above the surface, causing ripples across the water. The mayflies disappeared in one gulp. "Who do we have here then? Hmm, let me see now: two honey bees and a butterfly. Quite extraordinary, I have to say!" He seemed to be in a jolly mood which was a relief for his visitors.

"Which one of you bees did that mean old pike swallow on the way here? Didn't expect to end up in the belly of a fish today, did you?" He laughed a gurgling, fishy laugh at the thought of it, throwing back his head which made waves across the pool.

Deborah wondered how he could possibly know about the drama with the pike.

"Er, that was me, Sir," said Tadpole, looking down from his perch on Kite's head. "I wasn't inside the fish for very long though thanks to Kite.

He dived into the river to save me. You see, he's an expert at rescuing bees!" They all chuckled.

The Admiral noticed Emeth as she flew down next to Kite on the rock, her bright blue, yellowy-orange wings catching the sunlight. He asked, "And you young butterfly, you are local to the river. Am I correct?"

"Yes Sir, I am," replied Emeth. "My family has lived in the forest on the edge of the red poppy fields for many generations. It's a pleasure to meet you, Admiral Trutt."

"And what about you up there, what's your name?" the old fish asked Deborah, "Are you the one Kite told me about? I hear you're leading the search for your uncle. Speak up, my dear."

"Yes Sir, I am. My name is Deborah, and this is my brother, Tadpole. Our home is in Colonel

Hoot's tree far beyond the Big River. Uncle Albert left our nest in Bluebell Meadows a long time ago and never returned. We believe he is alive and may be living in this area. We have come here to find him and take him back to our colony."

"Of course, of course! So you must be Princess Deborah, Queen Miriam's daughter! Am I right?" It was a mystery how this ancient trout, who spent most of his life asleep, seemed to know about everyone and everything without ever leaving the pool.

"Yes, that's right Sir, but how do you know my mother?" she asked in awe of his great knowledge.

"Oh, that's easy," he replied with a smile. "Your friend Kite told me all about you this morning." He winked at Kite and made everyone laugh.

Now that the introductions were over, Deborah wanted to find out what the Admiral knew about her uncle. "Admiral Trutt, Kite said you have some information for me about Uncle Albert. We would like to find him as quickly as possible, and would be grateful for anything you can tell us."

So the Admiral described his encounter at the pool with Albert a few days earlier, and how he had sent him away because of his loud singing.

"Your uncle has a surprisingly strong singing voice for such a small creature! However, as I explained to him I cannot tolerate noise while I'm napping. Everyone around here knows that. Your uncle seems to be in a world of his own. Anyway, I asked him to buzz off and find another place to do his singing. Thankfully I haven't seen him since." The old fish yawned a big yawn and swam around the pool in a large circle, preparing for his afternoon nap.

Deborah was thrilled to hear this news. "So Uncle Albert was right here on this very rock just a few days ago? That's wonderful! It sounds just like him. He loves to sing! Thank you so much for your time, Admiral!"

The friends said goodbye to Salmo Trutt and he swam back down into the deep water, disappearing beneath the rock. They quietly left the pool and followed the river back to the sunflower meadows.

It was getting late in the day, and breakfast had been a long time ago. Deborah, Emeth, and Tadpole were tired and hungry. As soon as they reached the sunflowers, Emeth and the siblings began to visit one flower after another, enjoying a rich feast of nectar and pollen. Kite went fishing.

It was important for each of them to keep up their strength. No one knew how long their search would take. They were now certain that Uncle Albert was alive, but they still did not know exactly where to look for him. The Big River stretched for many miles and the old bee could be anywhere.

They needed to gather more information and find clues that would lead them to the missing bee.

CHAPTER 19
The Royal Palace of Sticks

After supper, the friends said goodbye to Emeth as she returned home to the poppy fields for the night. The siblings climbed up on Kite's back, which was now Tadpole's favorite way to travel everywhere they went. Kite soared up toward the eagles' nest which rested in the high branches of the pine tree.

The eagle king and queen were pleased to welcome the weary companions to their home. Kite's parents were delighted to see Deborah again. They were kind hosts, and they quickly made Tadpole feel like part of the family. The friends talked late into the evening, telling the royal couple all about their adventures on the river that day.

Just before they settled down to sleep, the eagle king requested to speak with Deborah and Tadpole.

"Deborah, you have been given an important assignment to find your uncle. As parents ourselves, we are concerned that Queen Miriam may be worried about young Tadpole and would want to know you are both safe. So with your permission, I would like to fly to Bluebell Meadows at first light to meet with your mother and assure her that you and your brother are safe here with us. This is something I can do for the rescue mission while you focus on finding your uncle. May I do this for you?"

Deborah was touched by the king's thoughtfulness. "Your Majesty, thank you for your kindness. Yes please, we would be very grateful if you would put Mother's mind at rest and let her know that Tadpole and I are safe. We also want to thank you for inviting us to spend this night with you. We feel protected and at home here which means a lot to us, doesn't it, Tad?" Deborah said looking with affection at her little brother.

"Oh yes, it does! Thank you, Your Royal Highnesses!" he spluttered, his big face beaming in wonder. Tadpole was completely in awe of the eagle king and queen. He could never have imagined he would be spending the night in a real eagle's nest.

Feeling brave he blurted out, "Er, King Eagle, when you see Mother tomorrow, please would you tell her that I'm sorry I left without asking and I forgot to do my chores first? And would you ask her to tell cousin Buzby that I'm staying the night in an eagles' nest? He won't believe me when I tell him!"

The royal couple glanced at each other. They were amused by the little bee's request.

"Of course, I will do that with pleasure, Tadpole," the king assured him. "Goodnight. And you may call me King Aquilla," he added with a sparkle in his eye.

Tadpole felt very special. Wowee—he was allowed to call the king by his real name! As the young bee tucked in under Kite's wing he was so full of joy. It took him a long while to fall asleep that night.

King Aquilla left the nest as dawn broke the next morning to fly to Bluebell Meadows. Deborah and Tadpole woke from a deep, restful sleep under their blanket of feathers. The friends had arranged to meet Emeth at the golden flowers, and it was time to go. They were looking forward to a feast of sweet nectar and pollen to start the day.

The siblings said goodbye to the eagle queen and climbed aboard Kite's back. He launched off the side of the nest and glided away from the tree, his friends holding tight to his feathers. As they approached the riverbank, Deborah felt hope rise within her that today could be the day they would find Uncle Albert.

Meanwhile, at Bluebell Meadows that same morning, Queen Miriam woke early from a troubled sleep. As soon as her eyes opened her thoughts turned immediately to her young daughter who was far away at the Big River. The queen had so many questions in her mind: Did she really do the right thing sending Princess Deborah on this mission of unknown dangers? Would they find Albert alive? How long would it take? And what had become of Tadpole? She had a hunch about where he went and tried not to worry about her son's mysterious disappearance.

The sun was rising over the mountains. The queen needed some fresh air before facing the royal duties of the colony. She made her way to the lookout platform at the entrance of the nest to watch and wait. Perhaps the fresh air would help her think more clearly.

This was her favorite time of day, before the hustle and bustle around the nest really began. She settled down on the platform, looking out to the distant horizon of trees and mountains bathed in the morning sunlight.

It was then she saw him. At first she thought it was Kite and her heart skipped a beat. The morning sun was in her eyes making it difficult to see. He was still a long way from the old tree, but as he came in closer she saw his great white head against the brown feathers of his large body. Who could it be?

She refused to panic as the elders and royal advisors rushed to the entrance to join her and find out if the rumors were true: an unknown eagle was approaching.

"My queen, what are your orders? Shall we call in the workers from the fields?" said one.

"It could be too late already. He's coming in fast!" said another.

They gathered around her nervously, looking to their queen for direction as the giant bird reached the nest.

"Stand firm everyone! There is nothing to be afraid of. An eagle has no quarrel with a colony of bees." Queen Miriam spoke with the calm confidence she had practiced for so long. In her heart however, she was feeling a little nervous.

King Aquilla landed on a branch close to the entrance and folded up his huge wings. He was a magnificent bird. His pure white head gleamed in the sunlight, and his feathers were smooth and perfectly preened, as was fitting for a royal king.

"I need to speak with Queen Miriam, if you please," he called out to the large swarm of bees that had gathered a safe distance from the unknown visitor. "I bring news of Princess Deborah and young Tadpole."

When she heard this, the queen gasped and told the elders, "Follow me!" as she flew up to greet the eagle.

"I am Queen Miriam, Sir, and these are my advisors and elders of the colony. We welcome you to our home." The older bees were nervous but bowed to honor the king of the skies.

"Thank you, Queen Miriam, you are most kind. I am Kite's father, King Aquila."

"Ah, it is a great honor to meet you," the queen replied. Now that she was closer, she could see the family resemblance.

"I am honored to meet you too, Queen Miriam. My queen and I have the greatest respect for you and your family. I came here today to let you know that your son Tadpole is safe. He is with Princess Deborah and Kite at the Big River. I am happy to report they are all doing well."

"Oh, that is welcome news. I have been concerned about Tadpole since his disappearance the day my daughter left here with Kite. As I suspected, he must have hidden somehow in Kite's feathers before they set off on their journey." She shook her head, smiling, and sighed, "He is so much like his sister—curious and headstrong. You have traveled a long way to put my mind at rest, and I thank you for your thoughtfulness."

The eagle king bowed his head in response.

The queen continued, "King Aquila, do you have news of the rescue mission?"

So the king told Queen Miriam and the elders how the search was going so far. He explained that Deborah's friend, Emeth, had joined the others at the sunflower meadows and told of their meeting with Admiral Trutt at the Quiet Pool. The queen was encouraged to hear that Albert had been seen there in the last few days.

King Aquilla was a wise king. He thought it best not to repeat the story of Tadpole being swallowed by the pike. After all, there was no need to worry the queen. No, he would leave that story for Princess Deborah to tell her mother once they were all safely back home.

"Queen Miriam, you can be proud of your brave daughter. Deborah is leading the rescue mission like a true princess. Please rest assured that my queen and I will be keeping an eye on the youngsters but will only intervene if it becomes absolutely necessary. They are all learning valuable lessons which will prepare them to rule and reign in life when their time comes."

As he was about to leave, King Aquilla remembered his promise to Tadpole. "Ah, yes, there is one more thing. I promised young Tadpole I would give you a message. Now let me see; first of all, he sends his apologies for not asking your permission to leave the nest, and for not completing his chores before he left."

The queen smiled, her mother's heart warmed by her son's apology.

The king continued, "He also asked if you would please let 'cousin Buzby' know that he is sleeping each night in our nest. Young Tadpole seems to be enjoying the experience very much. There, I believe I have delivered the full message."

With that, he bowed his white head in respect to the queen and her elders and launched off the branch, rising high in the sky to return home.

CHAPTER 20

The Search for Whisper

Back at the Big River, Deborah and Tadpole were eating breakfast while waiting for Emeth to arrive, and Kite took the opportunity to preen his feathers at the water's edge. It was a perfect day. The river flowed gently by, bubbling over the rocks in the shallows. The sheep were grazing on the lush grass, and every sunflower faced the morning sun in a blaze of golden yellow.

When Emeth arrived she was breathless. She could not wait to tell her friends about the events of the night before.

After greeting the siblings, she began, "On the way home last night, I saw my old friend, Whisper the hare. He lives in a fallen tree trunk beyond the poppy fields. He was fascinated to hear about our mission to find your uncle. I told him Albert was probably the only bee he would ever meet who loves to sing, and guess what, Deborah? Whisper knew exactly who I was talking about! In fact, he has seen your uncle recently!"

"So, we have another clue? Please tell us all you know!" Deborah asked eagerly.

Her wings quivering, Emeth continued, "Whisper said he was visiting a stretch of the river he had never been to before. As he was taking a drink, he heard a sound like singing, which caught his attention. He said it was unlike any birdsong he had ever heard, so he followed the sound along the riverbank. He could hardly believe what he saw—there was a honey bee standing on a white rock in the middle of the river, singing at the top of its voice! He had never heard of a singing bee and would love to meet your uncle. In fact, he offered to take us to the white rock today. Isn't that wonderful news?"

Deborah was delighted. Uncle Albert had been banished from the Quiet Pool, so it was possible he might return to sing at this same rock again.

"That is wonderful news, Emeth! There's no time to waste. Let's go find Whisper so he can take us to the white rock!" Deborah flew up from the flower, ready to leave the meadows.

"Wait, before we go, there is one more thing I must tell you," Emeth said, lowering her voice a little. She seemed to hesitate before sharing the rest of the news.

"Whisper reported that your uncle was surrounded by dragonflies—hundreds of them! He said he had never seen so many in one place before. And that's not all. It appeared that the dragonflies were dancing as your uncle sang for them!"

Tadpole could not believe his ears. Dancing dragonflies? It was unheard of! He had to see this for himself.

Deborah was astonished by the news too. It sounded very strange indeed. Dancing or not, dragonflies were dangerous predators, especially for bees and butterflies. She thought of her poor uncle surrounded by them. Uncle Albert could be in real trouble. She hoped they were not too late to save him, and she was thankful that Kite would be there to protect them.

So the four friends set off on their quest, following Emeth along a winding creek and across several meadows beyond the red poppy fields to look for Whisper. There was a lot of land to search, and the hare could be anywhere. So after a while, Kite had an idea to cover more ground.

He shared his idea with the others as they rested on a tree branch. "What do you think about us splitting up to look for the hare? It would be a lot easier for me to spot him from high in the sky. I can see for many miles from up there. You three could continue to search the poppy fields, and I could search from above. What do you think?"

Tadpole and Emeth quickly agreed to the plan. But Deborah was not so sure. For a while now she'd had the feeling they were being watched. However, she reluctantly agreed to Kite's plan, deciding it must be for the best. They had to find Whisper so he could lead them to her uncle.

Kite soared up to the heights, far above the trees to circle over the meadows. As Deborah watched him climb high in the sky, she was very aware that they were now unprotected.

The three friends continued to visit Whisper's favorite feeding grounds, but he was nowhere to be found. Eventually, Deborah stopped to rest and ponder what they should do next. All of a sudden, she remembered a lesson Colonel Hoot once taught her about hares. The old owl had explained that hares are nervous creatures, and if they see an eagle in the sky, they will run and hide. They will look for a safe place, like a hole or a hollow, and wait there until the eagle left the area.

Deborah said aloud, "Whisper must think he is in danger from Kite! No wonder we can't find him!"

She joined Emeth and Tadpole who were resting from the search on a leaf.

"I know why we can't find Whisper—he's afraid of eagles! Kite is flying over his territory, so he probably thinks he's in danger and has gone into hiding. We have to find a way to get Kite's attention and bring him back down here, or we may never find the white rock or Uncle Albert!"

As they were staring up into the sky looking for Kite, wondering what to do, suddenly a flash of blue and green appeared before them, taking the friends completely by surprise.

They were instantly face-to-face with danger in the form of a huge, fierce-looking dragonfly.

CHAPTER 21
Dart

The dragonfly hovered a few inches away from the three friends huddling together on the leaf. The much larger creature had four transparent wings that were moving faster than the eye could see. These wings made a terrible sound, like a thousand dry leaves rustling in a strong wind. The creature's long body was the color of the blue-green river shimmering in bright sunlight.

Deborah glanced up quickly to look for Kite and felt a sudden wave of fear as she realized they were alone to face this predator.

To be this close to a dragonfly was very dangerous indeed. Dragonflies are known to be extremely fast flying machines with a huge appetite and powerful jaws. Deborah knew there was no hope of escape using speed. No, they would need to stay calm and try to talk their way out of this encounter.

The brave princess placed herself between Tadpole and the dragonfly to protect her little brother, and Emeth came to her side in a show of  strength and unity. The menacing insect continued to stare and hover.

Deborah tried to sound calm and confident as she swallowed her fear. "Hello, can we help you?" she asked.

The dragonfly continued to stare and seemed to be enjoying a sense of power over these 'lesser insects.' "I don't know, can you?" it sneered, sarcastically.

"Perhaps if we knew what the problem was," said Deborah, ignoring the sarcasm. She thought, "Oh Kite, where are you?" Her mind raced to come up with a plan.

The predator replied in a very unfriendly manner, "Oh, there's no problem. I was just wondering what two bees and a butterfly are doing in my territory? That's all."

Just then, Tadpole pushed past his sister and piped up, "We have come here to find Whisper, and you're in our way, Mr. Dragonfly! My friend Kite will be here any minute and you'll be sorry you held us up!"

Tadpole didn't seem a bit afraid of the much bigger creature, who moved even closer to get a better look at the odd-shaped little bee.

"Well, well, well. Someone has a lot to say for himself. What's your name?" the dragonfly asked, now an inch away from Tadpole's face, it's wings sounding louder than ever.

"My name is Tadpole, and I don't like bullies!" he said, staring back into the dragonfly's huge eyes. He was either very brave or completely unaware of the danger he was in.

Emeth moved forward next to Tadpole and with her calming voice said, "We are here to find my friend Whisper the hare. Do you know him? We have an urgent matter to attend to and need his help."

The dragonfly now turned its attention to Emeth. "Oh, and what is so very urgent, Miss Butterfly, that you need the help of a hare? I can't wait to hear this!" he sneered at her with a mocking laugh.

Ignoring his rude behavior, Emeth replied patiently, "Well, Tadpole and Deborah's uncle went missing some time ago from their colony far beyond the river at Bluebell Meadows, and they have come here to find him. Whisper said he can lead us to the white rock where Uncle Albert likes to sing. You see, he's the singing bee. Perhaps you've heard of him?"

The previously unfriendly dragonfly stopped hovering and began darting around the three friends in all directions. Up and down, round and round he went until they all felt rather dizzy. They huddled closer together, not knowing what was causing this sudden change in behavior.

"Yes, of course, I know him!" he said, instantly losing all of his unfriendliness.

"Albert! He comes to sing for us down at White Rock! We all know him. We get together every afternoon at the river to dance to his songs. It's the highlight of our day. So Albert is your uncle?"

Deborah and the others were stunned. They looked at each other, utterly surprised. This was a very different dragonfly before them now. Perhaps he wasn't going to eat them after all?

Deborah, still trying to take it all in, answered, "Yes, he's our uncle! Are you saying he sings for you every day down at the river?"

"Yes! I don't usually like bees—nothing personal you understand, but we think your uncle is the 'bee's knees', pardon the pun! I'll take you there now if you like. It's not too far from here. It's the least I can do for Albert's family."

At that moment, Kite arrived, landing on a low branch in the tree above their heads. "Is everything all right, Deborah? Is this dragonfly bothering you?" he asked, ready to defend his friends.

"No, not at all. Actually, everything is great! He knows Uncle Albert and has offered to take us to the white rock. We couldn't find Whisper anywhere. Did you happen to see him from up there?" asked Deborah, relieved to see Kite. She always felt safe when he was around.

"Actually, I saw a couple of hares, but I didn't know which one was Whisper. I followed a brown one over several meadows until he disappeared into an old fallen tree trunk on the far side of the poppy fields. So I came back."

Deborah was right; the poor hare probably thought Kite was hunting him for breakfast!

She introduced Kite to the dragonfly. "This is our friend, Kite. He is helping us in our search for my uncle," she said.

The dragonfly flew like an arrow to Kite's perch on the branch. He was extremely fast.

"Hello, Kite! Good to meet you. My name is Dart," he said as he hovered in front of Kite's face. Dart had never seen an eagle up close before. The dragonfly continued, "Don't worry about finding Whisper. It would be my pleasure to escort you all to White Rock. Albert usually arrives sometime in the afternoon, so we can wait for him there. I'll introduce you to the Emperor when we get there. He's the big boss. When I tell him you are related to Albert, he'll make sure no one touches you. What he says goes. Come on, follow me!" And with that, Dart took off at high speed in the direction of the river.

Deborah, Tadpole, and Emeth wondered what it would be like to be surrounded by hundreds of dragonflies. Kite was aware that his friends were feeling anxious, and with good reason.

"Don't worry, I'll be there to keep you safe. Remember, it's my job to protect you all. I've done all right so far, haven't I?" he said with a smile, trying to reassure them.

The companions knew Kite would protect them, and they tried to relax, holding tight to his feathers as they followed Dart to the river.

Deborah and Tadpole could hardly believe it—they were on their way to be reunited with their long-lost uncle.

CHAPTER 22
Dragonflies Galore!

White Rock stood tall in the middle of the river, water frothing and splashing all around it. Whisper was right; there were hundreds of dragonflies here! It seemed like the entire dragonfly population was gathering in this place—and they kept on coming.

The noise made by thousands of dragonfly wings sounded like thunder!

It was very dangerous for a butterfly, bee, or any insect, to be so close to these predators. But Dart assured them that they were safe. The Emperor and his friends were there to dance, not to eat. As they arrived, Dart introduced Deborah and Tadpole to everyone as Albert's niece and nephew. The dragonflies were delighted to meet Albert's relatives. They were huge fans of the singing bee.

Dart called out, "Come on, it's time to meet the Emperor. Follow me!"

He led the way through the sea of dragonfly bodies, which parted in front of their guide. The three companions nervously followed behind Dart, feeling unsure if they were really safe or not. Kite stayed close by on the branch of a tree that overlooked the river, to keep an eye on his friends. He was ready for action if they needed his help.

The Emperor was hovering above the white rock, looking up and down the river, waiting for Albert to arrive. He was magnificent! The Emperor was much larger than Dart with a long, sky-blue body and four huge, yellowish wings. Several big dragonflies hovered around him, looking unfriendly and fierce.

The Emperor saw Deborah, Emeth, and Tadpole approaching the rock behind Dart. When he turned to face them, the friends could see that the dragonfly's eyes were bright green and so big that they appeared to cover his entire head! Tadpole could not take his eyes off this fearsome creature and stayed close to his sister. Emeth and Deborah exchanged a worried glance. The atmosphere was tense.

"Who do we have here then, Dart? Friends or food?" asked the Emperor as he circled around the companions. Deborah hoped that Dart would give him the right answer as she gulped down her rising fear.

Dart looked pleased with himself as he introduced his new friends. "They're friends, Boss. This is Deborah and Tadpole, Albert's niece and nephew, and their friend, Emeth. I found them out there beyond the poppy fields looking for

Albert. They came all the way from Bluebell Meadows to find him. The eagle's name is Kite. He's their guardian."

Dart had done a good job today keeping the boss informed of what was happening in his territory. The large dragonfly looked over at Kite whose eyes were fixed on the Emperor.

"I see," the Emperor said. "Well, in that case, welcome to White Rock! If you're Albert's family, you're friends of mine. Make yourselves at home. Your uncle is quite a celebrity around the river. Everyone loves the singing bee!"

He reassured his visitors, "Don't worry, my little friends, no one will harm you. Dart, tell the others these three are not to be eaten!" He threw his head back and laughed as he saw a look of relief appear on their faces. The tension lifted, and Deborah, Emeth, and Tadpole began to relax.

Deborah and the others returned to the riverbank to join Kite and wait for Uncle Albert. All the dragonflies were in awe of Kite. The poor eagle was surrounded by them! They had never met an eagle before, and they swarmed around him in a sea of crackling wings. Kite was overwhelmed by all the attention so Deborah came to his rescue, politely asking Dart's friends to give him some space. (She noticed that dragonflies do not seem to have many social skills.) Eventually, the dragonflies lost interest in their visitors, and everyone settled down to wait.

Tadpole could hardly keep still, he was so excited. He was very young when his uncle left the nest, too young to remember much about him. But Tadpole did remember hearing Uncle Albert sing. His uncle loved to visit the nursery and sing over the larvae and the growing bees. However, Albert was always shooed away by the nursery workers when they caught him because singing was strictly forbidden in the colony.

The afternoon stretched on, and Albert still didn't appear. The dragonflies began to murmur among themselves and became restless.

Deborah asked Dart, "What are they saying? Is something wrong?"

"We don't know," said her new friend." Albert is very late; he's usually here by now. The boss wants me to take a few friends down the river to look for him. You and the others stay here in case he shows up, okay? We won't be long."

So they waited and watched until Deborah and Tadpole could wait no longer. They had to do something to find their uncle.

Deborah turned to her friends. "Something's wrong, I can feel it. We can't sit around here doing nothing. Dart and the others went downstream to search, so let's go upstream and look around. Perhaps Uncle Albert needs our help."

So they climbed aboard Kite's back once again and set off up the river. The friends flew in silence for a while, looking and listening for clues—anything unusual along the riverbanks. Eventually, Kite landed on an old tree stump beside the water to listen. All was quiet apart from the sound of the breeze rustling in the treetops and the soft gurgling of the river passing by. The birds were singing. Everything seemed peaceful.

Then, all of a sudden, the shrill sound of screeching cut through the quiet afternoon. It was the frenzied squawking of birds—but not just any birds. Kite recognized this sound from his days as a young chick growing up in the eagles' nest. This noise was made by hungry magpies out hunting. He was certain of that.

"Come on! Let's go see what those birds are so excited about."

CHAPTER 23
The Rescue

The companions flew upstream toward the sound. Kite was on high alert. He took the job of protecting his friends seriously. The siblings and Emeth tightened their grip on Kite's feathers as they approached the next bend in the river.

Sure enough, there they were—the magpie twins! The black-eyed bullies were jumping around in the branches of a tree that leaned out over the water. They hopped from branch to branch, flapping and squawking loudly. Something had their full attention. The birds were focused on a large spider's web suspended above the river between two thinner branches.

As they approached the tree, Kite and his friends could see a small creature caught in the middle of the web. It was well and truly entangled in the strong threads. The bully birds were so engrossed in their sport of mocking the poor victim that they didn't notice Kite as he landed silently on a branch nearby.

"Quiet everyone," Kite whispered as they watched the scene in front of them.

Deborah and Emeth remembered the first time they met these beady-eyed brothers the day Kite was dangling from the pine tree. They tried to see what was holding the bird's attention.

With a gasp of horror, Deborah recognized the victim. There, caught in the sticky threads of the web, was Uncle Albert!

"It's him! It's Uncle Albert!" she whispered. "We have to do something quickly before it's too late!"

"Kite, look!" said Tadpole, "There's a spider! The spider is coming to get Uncle Albert!"

Sure enough, a large black spider had appeared from behind the tree trunk on the riverbank. It was crawling slowly along the branch toward the web, completely ignoring the two magpies. It had four hairy legs attached to each side of its fat, shiny body. When it reached the web it crawled to the center and stood over Albert, casting a dark shadow across its victim.

Kite was thinking fast. "I have a plan," he whispered. "We have the element of surprise right now. The birds don't know we're here yet. I'm going in to deal with those magpies and then come back for you as fast as I can. For your own safety stay here and keep out of sight."

Everyone agreed and huddled together on the branch as Kite launched his attack. With his eyes fixed on the target, the young eagle flew silently toward the magpie brothers who were still busy taunting Albert.

Then, letting out a loud screech like a war cry, Kite swooped in, knocking the first bird off its perch from behind with the weight of his large body. The unsuspecting creature did not have time to open its wings and fell headfirst into the river with a great splash!

Kite spun around and headed toward the second black-and-white bully. The frightened bird squawked loudly when he realized he was under attack. Leaping off the branch, he flew across the river as fast as he could to escape the eagle's talons, but he wasn't quick enough. Kite chased him down, catching hold of his tail feathers.

The young eagle dangled the magpie over the surface of the water, shaking the cowardly bird before dropping him into the river to join his brother.

"If I ever catch you two bullying anyone again, it will be for the very last time. Do you understand me? Now, get out of here and stay away from the Big River!"

Both birds were thrashing about in the water, trying to keep afloat. Kite watched as they made it to the far riverbank, wet and humiliated. The twins used the reeds and grasses to pull themselves up out of the water and onto the bank. Then, after a quick shake of their feathers, they took off for the forest as fast as their soggy wings could carry them.

After they left, Kite returned to pick up his friends.

"Kite! The spider!" cried Deborah, as they climbed on his back and flew to the web to rescue Uncle Albert. The spider was standing over the bee, protecting its prize. Kite landed as close as he could, aware that one wrong move could be fatal for Albert.

Just then, to everyone's surprise, Emeth fluttered down from her perch on Kite's back and spoke calmly to her friends, "Leave this to me."

With one flap of her beautiful wings she floated over to the spider's web, landing on a twig close to Albert. The friends watched in amazement to see what would happen next.

Emeth addressed the spider in a friendly but firm voice, "Excuse me, this bee you have in your web is a relative of my friends over there, and they would very much like you to let him go now. What do you say?"

The spider stared at Emeth in an unfriendly manner, then looked over at Deborah and Tadpole who were perched on Kite's shoulder.

"Why should I? He landed in my web, which means he's mine now," replied the spider, looking menacing as it hunched over its victim. Emeth was relieved to see that Uncle Albert was still alive. He looked weak and his eyes were glazed, but thankfully he was breathing.

"You see that eagle over there? You do realize he is more than capable of destroying you and your home and taking Uncle Albert away from you? That's his name, Albert, the one caught in your web. But you seem like a sensible spider who would want to live to see another day. Is that true?" Emeth asked politely.

The spider looked from Emeth to Kite and back again several times, trying to decide if the butterfly was bluffing.

Finally it replied, "The bee's almost dead, you know. It flew right into my web trying to escape those ridiculous birds. I didn't do a thing." The spider looked at Albert, drooling a little at the thought of supper.

With a calm confidence, Emeth said, "We're not blaming you—we just want our friend back. Now move away from the bee. Go on, and you won't get hurt."

The spider glanced over at Kite a few more times, its front legs lifting and lowering as it thought about the dilemma. That eagle could do some serious damage, for sure. It didn't like the look of his huge, curved beak. It wasn't worth the risk.

"Oh, take the old bee, see if I care. There's plenty more where that one came from," the spider said grumpily, reluctantly backing down. The black spider left Albert in the web and crept back along the branch toward the tree trunk, looking over its shoulder to keep an eye on Kite. Finally, it disappeared from sight.

Emeth returned to the others, "We need to move quickly. Albert is very weak. Kite, do you think you can pull him free from the web and carry him back to White Rock? I have an idea."

Kite nodded, opened his wings, and glided over to where Uncle Albert was cocooned in the sticky threads. Carefully and gently, he used his beak to lift the bee's entangled body away from the web.

Deborah flew up close to her uncle to reassure him. "Uncle, it's me, Deborah. Don't worry, you're safe now. The spider has gone and those mean magpies too." She could see he was struggling to breathe and wasn't sure if he could hear her.

"Uncle, we need to get this web off you as soon as possible, so hold on. We're going to get you some help." She turned to her friend.

"Emeth, what is your idea for getting Uncle Albert untangled?"

"Well, dragonflies have powerful jaws, that's why we're taught to avoid them. But those jaws are exactly what we need right now for cutting through these strong threads. I'm sure Dart and his friends would be more than happy to help. It's worth a try, don't you think?"

They all agreed to the plan and flew up on Kite's back, holding tight to his feathers. With the cocooned bee held gently in his beak, Kite launched up and away, flying down-river as fast as he could.

Tadpole was in awe of how Kite single-handedly dealt with the bully birds. "Wowee, Kite!" he exclaimed, "That was awesome! You really gave those bullies something to think about! They won't come back here in a hurry."

Deborah added, "And Emeth, you were amazing back there! You were very brave to confront that spider like you did. It was going to have Uncle Albert for supper!"

The friends were greatly relieved to have found Albert—and just in time to save his life.

Finally, they arrived at the stretch of river where the dragonflies were still waiting for the singing bee. Kite landed on the white rock and carefully set Albert down. The Emperor, along with Dart and his friends, gathered around the eagle to find out what had happened. Emeth flew down next to Albert's body and calmly began to give instruction to the dragonflies.

"There's no time to explain what happened right now. Albert is weak and can hardly breathe." She looked directly at the Emperor.

"Emperor Dragonfly, we need some of your best workers to get these threads off his body as quickly as possible. We need them to bite through the strands of web to set him free." Everyone looked anxiously from the Emperor to Albert, who was lying still on the rock before them.

The Emperor barked out his orders, "Come on! You heard the butterfly. Get to work!"

So, Dart and four big dragonflies huddled over the old bee, carefully chewing through the threads of web around Albert's body. Tadpole was fascinated and stayed close by to watch. Deborah and Emeth, on the other hand, could not bear to look and waited with Kite a short distance away.

There was silence on the rock as the dragonflies concentrated on their work. Was Uncle Albert strong enough to survive his ordeal?

Eventually, every single thread had been carefully removed from his body, and Uncle Albert was freed at last! Deborah came to his side as Dart and the others backed away to let her in. She could see his wings were badly crumpled and his legs were crooked, but thankfully he was still breathing.

"Uncle Albert, it's me, Deborah. Can you hear me, Uncle? Please open your eyes if you can hear me." They waited silently for a response.

Suddenly, one of Albert's crooked legs moved slightly, and he half-opened one eye. They all had been holding their breath, waiting for this moment. He moved! He was alive!

Dragonfly wings started beating with excitement. An explosion of cheering erupted around White Rock as they danced and twirled for joy. Kite joined in, stretching out his wings he lifted his great head and let out a celebration cry. Then everyone became still again to listen as Uncle Albert tried to say something to Deborah.

"My dear child... wha...what are you doing here so far from home?" he said in a whisper as he tried to move his legs to stand.

"Whoa, please don't try to get up, Uncle Albert," said Deborah. "I'll explain everything when you are feeling better, I promise. You have been through a lot, but we're here to help you now. That's it, lay still and rest." Albert had very little strength, and he took her advice.

Deborah knew they had to get him home to the colony to take care of him, but not tonight. He was far too weak to travel all that way tonight. No, he needed to eat and have a safe place to rest and regain some strength for the journey home.

Tomorrow would be soon enough to take Uncle Albert back to Bluebell Meadows.

CHAPTER 24
Uncle Albert's Song

The companions said goodbye to the Emperor and their friend, Dart, and thanked them again for what they had done for Albert. As the dragonflies began to leave White Rock, Deborah realized that kindness can come in all shapes and sizes, and enemies can become friends. These dragonflies, who are fearsome predators, showed great kindness today to Uncle Albert.

As she watched the swarm leave, Deborah and the others would never forget the deafening roar of many wings as they returned to their homes along the river in a display of vivid colors.

When all was quiet, Deborah looked down at her uncle's body lying still on the rock beside them. He had been through a terrible ordeal and she wanted to give him some hope and encouragement. The young princess thought for a moment, then moved closer. She had an idea.

"Uncle, do you remember the song you taught me when I was little? The one we used to sing together in the nursery when nobody else was around?" He remained motionless, breathing slowly. "You called it, "The Runny Honey Song," remember? It goes like this..." Her friends listened in awe as Deborah sang softly to Uncle Albert on the rock:

Sweet and runny honey days in
fields of flowers and trees,
Sunny days are honey days in the
life of busy bees.

Buzzy bees are busy bees, making
honey for our friends,
Golden yellow, sweet and yummy,
every bee loves runny honey!

*Runny honey is the best; it's sticky
and it's sweet,
It makes us strong to sing our song—
pure honey is a treat!*

To everyone's surprise, as Deborah finished the song, Albert lifted his head and gave her a weak smile. He knew the song very well. He had made up the words and the tune a long time ago for the young bees in the nursery. It comforted him to hear her singing it to him now. Fond memories of his life in the colony suddenly came flooding back.

It was a precious family moment and no one spoke—that is, until Tadpole became restless, as young bees do. "Sis, I am so-o-o hungry! Can we go now?" he asked brightly, thinking of his rumbling tummy. "Perhaps Uncle Albert can make it to the golden flowers so we can eat supper before dark?"

They were all feeling tired and hungry after the day's adventure. Kite nodded his agreement. He unfolded his wing to allow Deborah and Tadpole to carry their uncle up to rest between his shoulders. The siblings held on to his crumpled body, keeping him safely in place as Kite launched off the rock. The hungry adventurers headed downstream toward the sunflower meadows.

It was dusk as they arrived at the golden flowers, and the sun was low in the sky. Deborah, Emeth, and Tadpole carefully placed Uncle Albert in the center of a large sunflower. Deborah helped her uncle take a long drink of sweet nectar. Then they all tucked into the feast next to him. Kite took the opportunity to go fishing.

After supper the friends said goodbye to Emeth and arranged to meet her at first light for breakfast—it was to be their last day together at the Big River. Gradually, the sun disappeared behind the mountains and darkness fell over the meadows. It was time for Kite to take his friends up to the eagles' nest. They were all ready for a good night's sleep.

In the palace of sticks that night, Albert and his rescuers slept peacefully under the safety of Kite's wing. Just before sleep overtook her, Deborah thought back over the events of the day. As she lay there in the darkness, she felt a mixture of emotions: relief, joy and sadness—relief and joy that her uncle was alive and that they had found him in time, mixed with sadness over his crippled body. She was also sad that the rescue mission was almost over. Tomorrow, Deborah would have to say goodbye to her dear friend Emeth and to her life of freedom and adventure at the Big River. Soon she would be facing those "terrible princess lessons" and her royal responsibilities in the colony.

Deborah was grateful that no one was awake to see her tears as they fell onto Kite's feathers in the darkness.

CHAPTER 25
Fond Farewells

Kite woke as the sun rose to light up the new day. His parents had already left the nest to go fishing, and he decided he would join them before the journey back to the bee colony with Albert. But first, he would take his friends to meet Emeth for their final breakfast together.

He gently woke Deborah and her brother. "It's time to go," he said quietly.

No more words were needed. They all knew it would not be easy to say goodbye to the gentle butterfly who had become such a great friend.

Deborah shook the sleep from her body and looked over at Uncle Albert. His wings and legs were crumpled and twisted, but thankfully he was breathing peacefully. No one knew for sure if he would survive the long journey back to Bluebell Meadows, but they had to try. They had come too far to give up hope now.

As they approached the sunflower meadows that morning, Tadpole was the first to spot Emeth's colorful wings among the blanket of golden flowers.

"There she is, over there!" he said, excited to see her. She always made him feel special and included, like he belonged. They had become firm friends. After making sure Uncle Albert was resting safely feeding on a sunflower, Deborah and Tadpole joined Emeth. Kite left to meet his parents for a quick breakfast before the journey.

Emeth was her usual joyful self as they feasted together that morning. She was always in a good mood. "My dear friends, how I have loved our time together these past few days!" she said. "I will never forget our adventures as long as I live. Deborah, I have learned so much from you. You are a brave leader with a loyal heart. Nothing can stand in your way! You have shown me what it looks like to persevere, believe the best, and champion your family."

Turning to Tadpole, she continued, "And you, Prince Tadpole, you give me so much joy! You are bold and courageous, like your sister, and I admire your love for adventure!" With a twinkle in her eye, she added, "I want to be just like you when I grow up."

Tadpole's wings hummed with delight.

Deborah spoke with grace and appreciation for this beautiful butterfly. "Emeth, I am so glad we met! I don't know what I would have done without you by my side. I cannot thank you enough for your loyal support on this rescue mission.

Thank you for your true friendship and for being my guide. Your calm courage and wisdom gave me strength when I needed it. Tadpole and I will never forget you."

With one flap of her wings, Emeth rose up from the sunflower and hovered above her friends for a few moments. "I hope we will meet again, dear ones!" she called out, and floated away on the breeze over the flower meadows.

Sitting in silence, Deborah and Tadpole rested with their uncle, deep in thought and waited for Kite. It would soon be time to return to Bluebell Meadows and reunite Uncle Albert with his family.

PART 4

The Homecoming

CHAPTER 26
A Hero's Welcome

Queen Miriam woke early that morning from a restless sleep and made her way to the entrance of the nest. She wanted to hurry down the long hallways to the lookout platform where she could watch for Kite's return. But the queen knew she must remain calm and lead by example. All eyes were on her as leader of the colony. Every bee in the nest was waiting for the safe return of Princess Deborah and Tadpole, and for news of Albert.

Arriving at the entrance the queen took her position on the platform, her eyes scanning the skies above the treetops for any sign of the eagle who would bring her daughter and son home. The queen had come here each morning since Deborah left the nest. Would Kite arrive today? Had they found her missing brother? Was Albert alive?

The queen was trying not to be anxious. Worrying would not bring them home any quicker. King Aquila's visit had brought her some comfort. She was glad to know that Tadpole and Deborah were safe with Kite at the Big River.

Queen Miriam settled down to watch and wait. The morning sun felt warm on her face, and after a while she drifted into a light sleep.

All of a sudden, the queen was jolted awake by the sound of voices calling out from the meadows below,

"They're coming! They're coming!"

The queen shook herself awake and looked out across the valley.

The entire colony began swarming around the old tree, trying to see the eagle for themselves. It was difficult to see anything through the crowd, so she flew up to a higher branch for a better view.

Then Queen Miriam saw him. It was Kite! He was approaching the boundary line of the meadows, his broad wings carrying him swiftly to the old oak tree. The elders and royal advisors surrounded their queen to protect and support her in case the report from the eagle was not good news.

Kite glided in, landing on the same branch of the tree that his father had occupied the day before. Silence fell among the bees who swarmed around him. The only sound to be heard was the low humming of a thousand bee wings. All eyes were fixed on Kite.

Tadpole was the first to appear. Much to everyone's delight the young bee flew up from Kite's feathers to a roar of cheering from the crowd. Next, Princess Deborah followed her brother. The entire colony erupted with joy when they saw that the young adventurers had arrived home safely. It was a real hero's welcome.

Then Kite stretched out his wing, and the crowd grew silent again. Moving slowly and carefully, Deborah and Tadpole helped their uncle down to the safety of the branch, holding onto his injured body. Every bee in the colony began to celebrate wildly when they saw him, cheering the return of their long-lost relative. Albert was alive!

Queen Miriam could not hold back her tears. Joy and relief overwhelmed her at seeing her brother again. She joined her beloved family as they surrounded Albert, reunited at last. The elders watched the family reunion from a distance. Some of the older bees were trying to control their own emotions. They could hardly believe that this small rescue party had returned triumphant. Uncle Albert was back in the heart of his family!

The royal family stayed huddled together for several moments. Queen Miriam tried not to show it, but she was troubled by her brother's condition. He looked very weak. She gave instructions to the nearest worker bees to carry Albert to the entrance of the nest and wait for her there. Before she could tend to Albert, however, the queen had a great debt of thanks to express to the young eagle who had brought her daughter and son home to her.

Queen Miriam flew up to join Kite, who was enjoying the celebrations.

"Kite, my words could never be enough to tell you how grateful I am to you for protecting Deborah and Tadpole. How could I ever thank you? How could we ever thank you?" She turned to look at the joyful bees flying around them, celebrating the return of Albert and the royal siblings.

Kite's eyes were kind and honest as he replied, "It was my pleasure and honor to serve you and to help your daughter, Queen Miriam. Deborah is a very special young bee with the bravest heart—like her mother, I don't doubt."

He bowed his head toward the queen. "It is a privilege to call Princess Deborah my friend, and to be honest, I have grown pretty fond of young Tadpole too. He is becoming a fearless prince for sure!" he said.

The queen nodded graciously, feeling proud of her two brave adventurers. "I look forward to seeing you again, Kite," she replied. "Please know you are always welcome here to visit as often as you like. Now, please excuse me, I must go. My brother is in need of my care and attention."

Queen Miriam returned to the nest and directed the worker bees to bring Albert to the royal chambers. She wanted to know what had happened to him, but there would be time to ask questions later. What he needed now was plenty of rest and only the best royal jelly for the next few days so he could regain some strength.

Deborah and Tadpole were enjoying the hero's welcome and all the attention—especially Tadpole. The young bee felt very important indeed.

Deborah knew that Kite would soon be returning to his home at the Big River. It would be hard to say goodbye to such a faithful friend. How could she go back to "life as usual" in the colony, knowing she might never return to the Big River again? She tried to remain positive and cheerful. She did not want Kite to see her looking unhappy on this great day of celebration.

Deborah joined her friend. Kite was watching Tadpole, who was surrounded by an audience.

The young prince was loving every minute of it. All of his cousins listened in awe to his many stories, asking a million questions about the magpies, the trout, the pike, and the dragonflies.

Deborah sighed, "Kite, isn't this wonderful? Everyone is so happy. We did it, my friend—we rescued Uncle Albert and brought him home!"

Kite knew how Deborah must be feeling about saying goodbye. He felt the same way.

"Deborah, I know it's hard to part company after all we have been through together these past few days. I hate to say goodbye too—believe me. But now that I have seen you with your family, I realize that this is where you belong. Your family cares for you and needs you. I believe you are going to be a great queen and leader one day. I have no doubt about that. It's been an honor to serve you and to help you find your uncle. And I will come and visit you and you can tell me all about those 'terrible princess lessons'!" he said with a chuckle.

His words were genuine and warm. Kite always managed to cheer Deborah up. She was really going to miss him.

"Thank you, Kite," she said. "I will be looking forward to those visits! And thank you so much for everything. We could not have found Uncle Albert without you. Don't wait too long to come back, promise?"

"I promise I'll be back before you know it." And with that, he launched off the tree, his huge wings scattering bees in all directions.

"Bye, Tadpole!" he called out as he circled above the nest, "See you when I come back for a visit. Look after your sister for me, okay?"

Tadpole looked up from his audience just long enough to answer, "Okay, will do! 'Bye Kite! Thanks for saving my life and everything!"

Wide-eyed, Tadpole's cousins watched the eagle fly away from the tree, as he continued his story about being swallowed alive by a ginormous silver pike.

Meanwhile inside the nest, the worker bees laid Albert on the queen's own bed and left her alone with her brother in the royal chambers. She was shocked by what she saw; his wings were bent and his legs were crooked. It looked like he would never fly again.

The queen spoke quietly to him, "Albert, it's me, Miriam. Can you hear me?"

There was no response. She continued, hoping he would recognize her voice. "We are so happy to have you home, dear Albert. You must be exhausted. You've had such a long journey. What a story you'll have to tell us when you're feeling better."

The queen waited a few moments, but there was no response. Only his slow breathing told her he was still alive.

As Queen Miriam turned to leave, she thought she heard Albert say her name. It was no more than a whisper, so she lay down close to her brother to listen in case he spoke again.

"I'm here, Albert. I am with you," she assured him.

"Miriam...dear sister. I'm sorry I stayed away so long. Please, will you forgive me?"

"Oh Albert, Albert! I forgive you, of course I forgive you! Now please, there's no need to talk anymore. We'll have plenty of time to catch up when you feel stronger. Get some rest now. I'll be back later to check on you."

She gently touched his head with her wing and left the room, brushing the tears from her face.

CHAPTER 27
The Colonel's Wisdom

The next morning, Queen Miriam announced a day's holiday for the entire colony to celebrate the return of Albert to his family. Royal jelly and other sweet treats were served to every bee, young and old. The festivities continued all day long.

Deborah invited her good friend Colonel Hoot to the celebrations, and the old owl was pleased to accept. After his mid-afternoon nap, he left the hollow in the oak tree and glided down to his favorite branch near the entrance to the nest. Many worker bees were coming and going, enjoying their day off. News traveled fast in the colony, and it wasn't long before Deborah heard that her guest had arrived.

She greeted him with delight and joined him on the branch. She had missed his company very much.

"Colonel Hoot, how good of you to come!" Deborah exclaimed.

"Hello-o-o my dear! Thank you for your kind invitation. I wouldn't have missed it for the world! I heard from your mother that you ar-  rived home safely with young Tadpole, bringing Albert home with you. Wonderful news—well worth celebrating! I am looking forward to hearing the whole story. Please, tell me all about your grand adventure."

So Princess Deborah and Colonel Hoot spent the afternoon together. She shared with her friend all that took place at the Big River leading up to

Albert's dramatic rescue from the spider's web. The Colonel listened intently, his ears twitching from time to time. He was especially fascinated to hear how hundreds of dragonflies gathered at the white rock to dance. He had never heard of such unusual behavior in the world of insects, and he made a note to refer to his books that evening.

The sun was going down as Deborah finished her account of the rescue mission. Colonel Hoot was curious to know what his young friend had learned during her time at the Big River.

Deborah thought for a moment before answering, "Actually, while I was there a very surprising thing happened to me in the sunflower meadows one day. I'm not exactly sure if I can explain it, but I would love to share it with you, Colonel."

Of course the old owl was curious to hear. He listened quietly while the young princess tried as best she could to describe how the powerful urge to sing overcame her. Deborah told her friend how she had sung with the sunflowers.

"It was a song I had never even heard before. The song seemed to bubble up inside me, flowing from the flowers themselves. It was a strange yet wonderful experience. Afterwards, I knew that singing is meant to be an important part of my life. It was like I was awakened by this song. I am starting to believe that perhaps I have a gift to awaken others to their own sleeping song. Like Uncle Albert when he sang for the dragonflies—his singing awakened them to their gift of dance! The encounter with the sunflowers taught me that there is a song within each of us—a melody to be released." Deborah was relieved to share the unusual experience with her trusted friend. She knew the Colonel would understand.

"Ah, Deborah my dear, you have learned a wonderful life-lesson indeed! I am thrilled to hear of your encounter with the golden flowers. Not everyone experiences such an awakening in their lifetime.

"I remember long ago how much I loved to hear the songs that floated up from these meadows back when your grandmother, Rosemary, was queen. You honey bees have been blessed with a unique sound, that's for sure. It's quite extraordinary! I believe there is an ancient song of bees that needs to be revived in this colony." Colonel Hoot looked off into the distance remembering those beautiful songs.

Deborah stared at her friend in amazement. "Colonel, you just said something about reviving the 'ancient song of bees'. Those exact words were part of the song I sang with the sunflowers! Please tell me what you know about this ancient song.

What does it mean?"

"Well you see, my dear, there is a song of nature that has always existed since The Beginning. The Creator made it to be that way. You could call it, The Poetry of Creation. It's like a dormant seed embedded within us all, but not all are awakened to it.

"For example, when your uncle sang his melody at the Quiet Pool, the Admiral sent him away. He did not want to hear it, unlike the dragonflies who heard his songs and responded with dance! You never know who will be awakened as you release your own song, Deborah. I encourage you to keep seeking and keep believing, and the answers will come to you."

Deborah pondered his words. They were full of wisdom beyond her understanding right now. But she sensed in her heart that it was alright not to understand everything all at once. She was willing to trust that in time she would learn more about the 'ancient song of bees.'

Deborah wanted to share something else with her friend, something that was heavy on her heart. She needed Colonel Hoot's wisdom and advice.

"Now that I'm back in the colony, I don't know what to do because there is no freedom to sing here. I cannot use this gift I've been given and that makes me sad. We have to bring songs back to the nest, but I don't know how. I'm afraid Mother won't listen to me, and anyway, the elders are set against it.

"Colonel, you have a long history of friendship with my family. Do you know the reason why singing was banned in our nest? It doesn't make any sense to me, and I cannot imagine living here for the rest of my life without the freedom to sing."

The old owl ruffled his feathers and blinked his big, round eyes. He knew the real reason why singing had been banned in the colony. Queen Miriam had told him the whole tragic story long ago. But it wasn't his place to tell the young princess. That was something only her mother should do.

"Ah, yes. Well, all I will tell you Deborah, is that a long time ago something terrible did happen in the nest. It caused your grandmother, Queen Rosemary, to forbid all singing. I only wish that I could have helped the colony on that tragic day, but it happened early one morning while I was still sound asleep. Sadly, when your family needed me the most, I wasn't able to help them." The old owl sighed.

"But what happened, Colonel? What took place here? I have to know."

"My dear, it is not my place to tell you. But I sense that it is time for the truth to be told now that Albert has returned to the nest. Here is my advice: talk with your mother, and tell her how you feel about singing now that the passion has been awakened in you. Ask her to explain what took place here—I'm certain she will help you to understand everything. Then, you must trust her as your mother and leader to make the right decision for the colony. She is a good queen. She will know what to do."

Deborah accepted the owl's words of wisdom. She believed he was right about her mother. "Thank you, Colonel Hoot," she said in response. "I will look for an opportunity to speak with her about it. I'll be starting my terrible princess lessons soon, so mother and I will be spending lots of time together!" she laughed, trying to lighten the conversation.

With great affection, the old owl replied, "Your mother made the right decision sending you and Kite to bring your uncle home. I am very proud of you, Deborah. I see the same qualities in you that I see in her, and saw in your grandmother before her. You are a noble queen-in-the-making with a good and courageous heart. You already have what it takes within you to lead this colony one day."

He stretched his wings as he continued, "And... I have a feeling that these princess lessons you are dreading won't be nearly as 'terrible' as you think. You never know, you may even enjoy the experience!"

Deborah doubted it but was grateful for the encouragement and wisdom.

Colonel Hoot continued, "Anyway, my dear, I am always here for you if you need me. You know that." Deborah knew that very well.

"Now please excuse me, it's time for me to go. The light is fading, and I have some preparations to make before my visit to the forest tonight. I have important business there and need to consult my books."

He opened his wings ready to leave. "There have been reports of a creature that has not been seen in this land for a long, long time. It's known as a pangolin. Did you ever hear of such a creature?"

Deborah smiled, knowing Colonel Hoot's love for learning about the rare animals of the Ancient Forest. The princess had not heard of this creature, and for a moment, she wondered what a pangolin might look like, but she decided not to ask. There was much to be done before the evening celebrations, and she had promised to help her mother get Uncle Albert ready for the banquet.

At that moment, Tadpole burst through the leaves, flying at top speed, giving his sister and the old bird quite a fright.

"Tadpole! How many times do I have to tell you, please slow down!" she said to her brother as he buzzed all around, making them both feel dizzy.

"Hi, Colonel!" said Tadpole, talking fast. "Hey, Sis, Mother sent me to find you. She needs your help getting Uncle ready for tonight. Come on! Last one to the throne room is a wasp! Catch me if you can! 'Bye Colonel!"

As quick as a flash, the young bee disappeared. Colonel Hoot was greatly amused by Tadpole's flying visit. His head went back as he let out his deep owl laugh.

"Hoooo! Hoooo! Young Tadpole is full of energy today! He's like a whirlwind! What has your mother been feeding that youngster?"

Deborah laughed too. "I think he got used to riding on Kite's back while we were away," she remarked. "He's been flying around at top speed ever since we got home. And he's also been eating sweet treats all afternoon!"

Deborah and the Colonel parted company as the sun was setting behind the mountains. She followed her brother into the nest to prepare for the great banquet, and Colonel Hoot returned to his home in the heart of the tree.

CHAPTER 28
The Banquet

That evening a special feast was arranged to celebrate the return of the queen's brother. Princess Deborah, Tadpole, and Uncle Albert were the guests of honor.

The dinner guests took their places at the long banqueting table, all looking forward to this grand occasion. Everyone rose from their place and bowed as Queen Miriam entered the throne room with her sister, Primrose. Albert was carried in on a special bed made from beeswax and covered with a blanket of moss. The queen wanted her brother to be as comfortable as possible during the celebration feast. Tadpole and Deborah were at his side.

Elder Cranberry was there, even though he disapproved entirely of the banquet. What nonsense! He was not in favor of the day's holiday either. It was a waste of valuable time to give every worker bee a day off from their duties in the meadows. Winter would come soon enough. The workers needed to make enough honey to see them through the cold months ahead, when the flowers would be gone and nectar scarce.

Queen Miriam was aware that some of her older advisors did not approve of giving the worker bees a day off. They never liked change, but she wasn't going to let that stop her from celebrating her brother's return home.

The feasting began. The banqueting table was overflowing with delicious honey, bee bread, royal jelly, and nectar juice. Tadpole's face was covered in runny honey in no time, and he ate till his tummy was more than full.

After dinner, the queen requested that the royal siblings share their stories of the rescue mission.

So Deborah began by describing the great beauty of the Big River and the sunflower meadows and how she met Emeth who had joined them in the search for their uncle. The dinner guests were riveted as she told the story of the silver pike who swallowed Tadpole, and how Kite bravely plunged into the water to rescue him, catching the fish in his talons. Then Deborah told of the meeting at the Quiet Pool with Admiral Trutt to find out what he knew about Albert, and of how they all stayed in the royal eagles' nest at night with the eagle king and queen.

Deborah described their face-to-face encounter with the fierce-looking dragonfly. She told how Dart quickly became a friend when he realized that Albert was their uncle, and he took them to White Rock to meet the Emperor, where there were hundreds of dragonflies waiting for Albert. Every bee was enthralled by the story as they heard how the search party eventually found Uncle Albert trapped in the spider's web, wrapped in sticky threads.

At this point, Tadpole took over the story and told how Kite chased off the magpie brothers and Emeth bravely confronted the spider who wanted to eat their uncle. The young bee was delighted to describe in great detail how the dragonflies had cut through the threads of the spider's web with their sharp jaws to set Uncle Albert free. Tadpole's big face was glowing as he painted the scene with his words, keeping his audience on the edge of their seats.

The bees around the banquet table listened wide-eyed and astonished. Even Elder Cranberry seemed to be attentive to the details of the Big River adventure.

Queen Miriam was so proud of Deborah and Tadpole. They had rescued their uncle and faced many dangers—dangers she hoped no one else at the feast would ever have to face.

The queen rose from her throne and went to her brother's side.

"Dearest Albert," she began, "I speak for the whole colony when I say it is a dream come true to have you safely back with us. It must have been lonely for you so far from home in such a hostile land. You survived a terrible ordeal at the Big River and have faced many formidable enemies like the magpies, dragonflies and the spider. Please would you tell us about your life there before you were rescued."

Albert's answer stunned them all. He gathered his strength and replied, "It was simply wonderful."

Every bee gasped in surprise. Elder Cranberry could not contain himself.

"Wonderful? How was it wonderful? From what they just described, the Big River sounds like a terrible place full of dangerous predators!"

The elders murmured among themselves, trying to understand what Albert meant by "wonderful." Had he lost his mind from being alone for so long in a strange land?

Albert continued, his voice sounding a little stronger now, "It was wonderful because I was free. For the first time, I began to believe that I was born to sing. I think I always knew it deep down, but being free to sing at the Big River made everything much clearer. Singing has been banned in this colony for a long time, as we all know. To live here where no songs could be sung again seemed unbearable to me—far worse than the dangers at the Big River. The dragonflies they spoke of were not my enemies; they were my friends. In fact, they were my audience! The Emperor, Dart, and all the other dragonflies looked forward to hearing me sing every single day. My songs released their gift of dance."

The guests were speechless. They could not understand what Albert was saying. Dancing dragonflies? No one had ever heard of such things!

The old bee continued, full of passion now, "Yes, the dangers at the Big River are real. As you can all see, I am crippled—my wings are useless and I may never fly again. But I won't let that stop me from singing! If I have to, I will find a place to live where songs are welcomed and appreciated, even if I have to crawl on these crooked legs to get there!"

Elder Cranberry could not keep silent. He exploded in a loud voice, "Singing? Bah! May I remind you, Albert, that this matter was settled a long time ago, before you left for the Big River. All the elders agreed that singing was bad for the colony. It keeps the workers from their work; it's a distraction, a nuisance—it serves no purpose whatsoever!"

The elder's face became angry and twisted as he spoke. His wings beat the air frantically, causing him to rise up from the banqueting table above them all.

Queen Miriam had heard enough. She spoke firmly, "That will do, Elder Cranberry! You will not speak to my brother that way, do you understand?" She tried to keep calm on the outside, but inside she was boiling with anger. The queen felt very protective of her brother.

The elder glared at everyone, then flew like an arrow out of the double doors of the throne room, which slammed behind him. An awkward silence fell as everyone wondered what was going to happen next.

The queen turned to her brother, full of concern, and said, "Albert, my dear Albert, I had no idea you felt that way. I knew you loved to sing when we were young. But, are you saying that the real reason you left the nest is because you were not allowed to sing anymore? Your passion for singing took you away from us, because we took the freedom to sing away from you? Oh, Albert, I'm so sorry, please forgive me!"

Albert reached out a crumpled wing towards his sister and said gently, "Shh, Miriam, it's okay, it's okay. It's just the way it was. The elders made their decision long before you were queen. They didn't want singing in the colony and I couldn't face life here without the freedom to sing. It's that simple. So I let you believe I wanted to go to the Big River to scout out the golden flowers. It was my  excuse to leave. I didn't have the courage to tell you I wasn't coming back. At the time it seemed like no one would understand."

"I understand, Uncle Albert," said Deborah, her heart beating wildly. "You see, while I was at the Big River, I discovered that I too have a passion to sing."

All eyes were now on the young princess. She looked around the room at everyone, searching for the right words to say.

"Singing is part of who I am," she said with confidence. "The truth is, there is a melody within each one of us. My uncle taught me that when I was very young. While I was at the Big River, I was awakened to the gift of song like never before. I believe we made a big mistake when the elders took the right to sing away from the colony."

There was a shocked silence as Deborah turned to the queen. "Mother, we must allow this gift to return to our family, to our workers, and to this colony! Singing is good for us all, young and old. We must teach our little ones to believe they have a unique song in their hearts. We need to raise our bees to enjoy their lives. It's good to work hard, but our lives cannot only be about working hard till we're too old to work anymore!"

Her mother listened in awe as her daughter spoke these words of wisdom far beyond her years. The queen remembered times in her own young life when she connected to her heart's song. Queen Miriam treasured those moments as some of her fondest memories as a princess growing up in the nest. She also remembered feeling the pressure of daily princess lessons, learning to value hard work above all else. Singing had been a wonderful escape from those pressures.

As those memories came flooding back, things were becoming clearer in the queen's mind. She knew this was an important moment.

She gathered her thoughts and spoke from her heart, "Elders, royal advisors, friends, family. This evening is a celebration of my brother's safe return to the colony, and we will continue to celebrate and be thankful. But we must take to heart what has been spoken here tonight.

"Princess Deborah and Albert, I want to thank you for reminding us all of the importance of the gift we each carry inside—the gift of our own unique melody. I believe, as you do, that we all have a song to sing. All we need is permission to let that song out for the world to hear."

The queen's words hung in the air. She sensed that the song inside of her had been buried for far too long under the heavy weight of royal responsibility.

Princess Deborah held her breath in the silence that followed. She knew that this was the moment to ask her mother to explain the real reason singing was forbidden long ago.

It was time to discover the truth.

CHAPTER 29
The Truth is Told

The royal chamber was quiet as Deborah gathered her courage.

"Mother," she continued, "if you believe in the gift of song, why was singing ever forbidden here? What happened? The elders have always told us that singing distracts the worker bees from their work, but that doesn't make any sense to me. Singing was always a part of our history—it's our inheritance. And as heir to the throne of this colony, I need to know the truth."

Queen Miriam knew that the real reason should not be hidden any longer. Deborah was right; it was far too important to be ignored. So the queen began to tell of the tragic events that led to the end of singing in the nest.

Many years ago, when Queen Miriam's mother, Rosemary, reigned as queen, Elder Cranberry and some of the older bees had served as her advisors. Queen Rosemary had been a good queen who loved her workers and treated them well and with respect. She encouraged the bees to sing freely as they worked, and every summer they produced plenty of honey. The bees were happy in their work and felt valued. They loved their queen and did their best each day to serve her well.

Then, one morning in late autumn, a raiding swarm of hornets came from the Ancient Forest and attacked the nest to steal the honey. These insects, much larger than the honey bees, showed no mercy. They raided their food supplies and killed any worker bees who tried to stop them. Many lives were lost, and it was a time of great sadness for the colony. Added to that loss, winter was approaching, and the stores of honey needed for the cold months ahead were all but gone.

One of the young worker bees who lost his life that day was named Toby. He had been like a son to Elder Cranberry. Toby had a unique gift of singing and a talent to create songs like no one else. Elder Cranberry used to say that Toby had the most beautiful singing voice he had ever heard.

The older bee never recovered from losing his talented young friend, and from that day on he could not tolerate the sound of singing in the nest. Singing was a constant reminder of Toby. Even the songs of mourning sung by the bees after the attack were too much for him to bear. So ever since that terrible day, Elder Cranberry's grief had caused his heart to become hard and bitter.

Not long after that dreadful day, Elder Cranberry gathered the royal advisors and elders together in secret. He convinced them that the hornets had attacked the nest because they heard the bees singing in the meadows. He said that the sound of singing was to blame for the hornets finding the honey! This was simply not true, but he could think of no other way to put an end to the songs which tormented him and constantly reminded him of his great loss.

The royal advisors believed Elder Cranberry. In their own grief, they also wanted something to blame for the tragic loss of lives. So every one of them agreed: to keep the colony safe, singing must be banned immediately.

The elders called an emergency meeting with their queen and told her what they now believed to be true; that the hornets invaded the colony, drawn by the sound of the singing bees. Queen

Rosemary was overcome by guilt. She had always encouraged the worker bees to sing, and she blamed herself for what had happened. So Queen Rosemary agreed to make a royal decree; from that day on, all singing was forbidden in and around the nest.

Deborah listened with tears in her eyes as Queen Miriam continued, "After the royal decree was made, the tragedy of the hornet's attack was simply too painful for Elder Cranberry and the elders to explain. So, when anyone asked why singing was forbidden, all the elders agreed to tell future generations that singing was banned because it 'distracted the worker bees from their work.' We have heard this said for so long now that every bee in the colony believes this is the true reason."

Queen Miriam sighed. She could see clearly now that the elders' decision had been a mistake. All it had achieved was deceiving the bees and stealing away the joy of singing.

Deborah was trying to fully understand. "So Elder Cranberry lied to everyone because his heart was hurt, and in his grief, he did not want to be reminded of Toby by hearing the sound of singing?"

The truth had been covered up for almost two generations—singing had been silenced by a lie.

The queen nodded sadly and replied, "Yes, that is the truth. But what you also need to know, Deborah, is that before the hornet's attack, Elder Cranberry had been appointed as the teacher of song by your grandmother. He had the most wonderful singing voice and was a very gifted singing tutor before he ever became an elder. He loved to encourage the gifts he saw in his students of all ages. That is how he became so fond of Toby. My mother once told me that Elder Cranberry would spend hours each day with Toby. He was training him in the hope that one day he would become the next teacher of song in the colony. Elder Cranberry wanted Toby to follow in his footsteps."

Tadpole had been listening intently, fascinated by the story. He could hardly believe what he was hearing.

"Wowee, Mother!" he exclaimed. "Elder Cranberry can sing? So you mean he hasn't always been grouchy?"

"No, Tadpole, he hasn't always been so unhappy," his mother replied, remembering the old bee before that tragic day. "Elder Cranberry was once a joyful bee like you, who was passionate about singing and loved to teach the little ones.

"There is one more thing you both need to know. Your uncle and I were young bees in the nursery the day the attack happened. My mother told me that Elder Cranberry had stayed with the youngsters to protect us from the hornets. The nursery workers fled in fear, but he refused to abandon us. Elder Cranberry blocked the doorway with his own body to keep us safe. I will always be grateful to him for that."

Deborah was astonished by the truth that was unfolding. "Wow, I had no idea that Elder Cranberry had so much courage," she remarked. "So, does that mean that Elder Cranberry taught both you and Uncle Albert to sing when you were growing up in the nursery?"

The queen replied, "That's right. It was his gifted teaching and love for song that first awakened our love for singing."

Deborah and Tadpole were beginning to see that there was a lot more to Elder Cranberry than they could have ever imagined.

Queen Miriam was relieved to finally tell the whole story. There were no more secrets to hide. The queen began to realize she and the colony had been living under the weight of rules and striving for too long. She had forgotten how to enjoy her life, and she knew the same was true for her workers. The elders kept pushing the worker bees to produce more and more honey each year, fearful of not having enough. They treated them like slaves instead of valuing them as family. The workers were the ones who kept the colony going. They had the right to enjoy their daily tasks—to sing freely and enjoy days off on special occasions.

The queen looked slowly around the room at the familiar faces staring back at her. Now that she had shared the truth, there was something important she had to do before this evening was over. She had never been more certain of anything in her life.

Queen Miriam spoke calmly, with royal authority, "So friends, that is the whole truth behind my mother's decision to ban singing in this nest. Queen Rosemary believed she was protecting the colony, and I honor her for that. However, I believe that today is the day to reverse that decision. Therefore, with the authority I have been given as your queen, I decree and declare that the bees of the Bluebell Meadow colony have the freedom to sing once again!"

Everyone gasped with shock at this royal declaration. Their queen had never decreed anything without the approval of the elders. She was breaking the rules of royal protocol, and every bee in the room knew it. There was an outbreak of murmuring among the elders.

Deborah, Tadpole, and Uncle Albert could not have been happier. Albert forgot all about his crooked legs for a moment and tried to jump for joy on his bed! Fortunately, Deborah was close by to steady him as they celebrated this wonderful moment together. Tadpole leapt up and began to fly around the room like a joyful whirlwind. He was joined by many others who were excited to receive the freedom to sing. This was the best homecoming gift the siblings could have imagined!

The celebrations continued late into the evening until all the food was gone and every bee was exhausted.

As Queen Miriam lay down to sleep that night, she thought about the events of the evening and all that had just happened. The changes made tonight were long overdue. Life in the colony was never going to be the same again.

As she lay alone in the darkness, the melody of a special song from long ago floated across her mind. She couldn't quite remember the words or how she even knew the song. The words were something about "nature's chorus" and "reviving the ancient song of bees."

She hummed the tune quietly as she drifted into the most peaceful sleep she'd had in a very long time.

CHAPTER 30
The New Teacher of Song

The next morning, Deborah and Tadpole woke up early. Today was an exciting new day for the colony. Last night's royal decree meant that singing was once again permitted, and it was time to take action. Deborah could not wait to share her gift of singing with the young bees, just as her uncle had done with her at their age. So with Queen Miriam's permission, she arranged a visit to the nursery and asked Tadpole to join her.

There was great excitement when the siblings arrived that morning. Princess Deborah and Tadpole had become celebrities overnight. They were heroes of the colony, having returned from the Big River with their long-lost uncle. Eventually, the little bees calmed down and were curious to learn whatever it was the royal siblings came to teach them. All eyes were fixed on their special visitors.

Deborah explained that they had come to teach the young bees about singing. But no one knew what singing was. They had never heard a song or sang a tune before. So Tadpole suggested they should begin with a demonstration.

"Hey Sis," he said, "let's sing the Runny Honey Song for them! They will soon pick it up. Come on, start us off!" He told the little ones, "She's a really good singer you know."

Deborah agreed and cleared her throat. "Thank you, Tadpole. The song we are about to sing for you is one my Uncle Albert taught me a long time ago, when I was growing up in the nursery like you are today. It goes like this..."

The young princess opened her mouth and started to sing like she had never sung before. She felt a flood of freedom explode from within as the words and familiar tune poured out. Tadpole joined in with great enthusiasm

Deborah encouraged the young bees, "It's easy to sing, so everyone can join in. Come on, that's it!"

They sang the song over and over so the bees could learn the words and the tune.

It wasn't long at all before every bee was joining in the song, their young voices filling the air. This was a brand new experience for these little ones, and they were enjoying every moment. Deborah could not be happier that the song her uncle once taught her in secret was now being sung openly. It was so much fun! She found herself making up another verse to sing,

> *Young bees, you're free to sing your song.*
> *Let's sing together all day long!*
> *No one can take your gift away—*
> *Like Runny Honey, it's here to stay!*

Everyone cheered and sang even louder. The young bees formed a line behind Deborah, singing at the top of their voices as she led them around the room.

They were having so much fun that no one even noticed when Queen Miriam and Albert entered the nursery. (Albert was feeling much better and was getting used to being carried around on his mossy bed by a team of worker bees). The older sister and brother stood quietly at the back and watched with delight as the younger sister and brother led the youngsters in a happy procession.

When the singing finally came to an end, the little bees flopped down exhausted, and the nursery workers announced nap time.

Queen Miriam went to congratulate her daughter, saying, "Deborah, that was wonderful, well done! You have a lovely singing voice, my dear, and you clearly have a gift with the young ones. Do you have a moment? Your uncle and I would like to talk to you."

Deborah left Tadpole with the youngsters, and joined her mother and Uncle Albert. Her uncle seemed to be excited about something and kept looking at his sister with a knowing smile, as if they shared a secret.

Deborah was curious, "Mother, what is it? What do you want to talk to me about?"

"Well, your uncle came to me this morning with a very interesting idea—an idea I like very much. Now that singing is being restored to the workers and encouraged in all of us, we will need someone who has a special gift of song to instruct our growing bees. Your uncle and I believe that you are the perfect one for the job. Deborah, I have come to ask you on behalf of the colony if you would consider the role of Teacher of Song for our young bees?"

Queen Miriam looked into her daughter's eyes, which were now brimming with tears.

"We believe in you, Deborah," the queen went on. "We have always believed in you. We want to give you this opportunity to grow in your gifting and encourage your passion for singing. My dear, I know you are not looking forward to starting your princess lessons, so I have suggested to the elders that teaching the youngsters to sing can become part of your training as future queen. As you teach, you will be learning how to lead and value your students, how to organize, and how to bring out the unique singing gifts in each one. These are important lessons to learn in the art of good leadership."

Uncle Albert was glowing with pride for his young niece. "Deborah," he said, "you have what it takes to do this. It's important that these young bees are awakened at an early age like you were. They each carry a unique and valuable song and like a seed planted on the inside, that song needs to bloom. You, my dear, are a natural-born teacher and you can help to bring those seeds to life."

Deborah was overwhelmed and overjoyed. She did not have to think about her answer; she was delighted to accept. These young bees would grow up with the freedom to sing and learn the value of their own song. And maybe teaching these little ones to sing would become part of reviving the 'ancient song of bees'!

Oh, how she wished she could share her wonderful news with Kite and Emeth!

Deborah sensed she had been prepared for this moment. She was born to do this. She also realized that she would need some help.

After thanking her mother and uncle, Deborah was returning to her chamber when she had an idea. She had been thinking a lot about Elder Cranberry and everything her mother had shared the night before. She had always thought of him as a grumpy old bee who did not understand the younger generation. Deborah now knew she had been wrong to judge him. She had not known his story.

She decided it was time to speak with him, so instead of going to her chamber she set off down the long hallway toward his room.

Deborah hovered outside the elders' door for a moment to gather her courage. What if the old bee refused to talk to her or became angry? She decided it was worth the risk, took a deep breath and knocked.

"Yes, what do you want?" he shouted from inside the chamber, sounding grumpy as usual.

"It's me, Princess Deborah, Elder Cranberry. May I speak with you please?"

There was a long pause, followed by shuffling noises, and finally the door swung open.

His face wrinkled into a frown as he stared at her, seemingly annoyed by the interruption.

Suddenly, before she had time to change her mind and leave, she blurted out, "I'm sorry for what happened to Toby."

Oh dear, she thought, that wasn't exactly how she meant to start the conversation. The frown was quickly replaced by a look of total surprise. Then there was an awkward silence.

"You had better come in," he said at last, looking up and down the hallway in case anyone overheard.

Once inside he closed the door and asked, "How do you know about ...T-T-Toby?" It was still hard for him to say the name after all this time.

"Mother explained last night after you left the banquet," Deborah said. "She told us the truth of what happened, and the real reason why singing was banned in the colony. I know the whole story, Elder Cranberry." She felt compassion for the older bee.

"She did, did she?" he replied. "Hmph. I suppose you've come to gloat, now that singing is allowed again. I heard the news this morning."

"No, I haven't come to gloat," Deborah clarified, "and I'm sorry you would think that of me," she said, trying not to be hurt by his comment. "There are two reasons why I came to see you. One is to say that I'm sorry for your loss. I had no idea."

Elder Cranberry looked down. He felt ashamed for speaking to the young princess that way. "Thank you," he said. "And what is the other reason that brings you here, may I ask?"

"Mother said you used to teach singing to the young bees a long time ago, and that is how you came to know Toby. I've come to ask you if you would be willing to help me? You see, this morning Mother offered me the position of singing tutor for the young ones in the nursery, which I have accepted. I don't have any experience in teaching, and I would really value having a mentor like you to help me. Would you consider sharing your wisdom and teaching experience with me?"

Deborah had no idea how he was going to respond. She waited, feeling nervous.

The old bee seemed to be having a moment of inner turmoil. There was a long pause before Elder Cranberry spoke again,

"Well, I... er... well, I don't know what to say. I haven't taught singing for a very long time, you know. Not since that tragic day. Your request is very unexpected. It's completely out of the blue. I really don't know what to think."

Deborah spoke kindly, with compassion, "Of course, you don't have to make a decision right now. I realize it's a lot to ask. But I want you to know that it would be an honor to have you as my mentor. I would value whatever help you can offer, and I know the young bees could learn so much from you. Will you think about it, Elder Cranberry? Please?"

This old bee had been short-tempered with her on many occasions, but now Deborah could see past his crusty outer shell. She believed that once he found his passion for singing again, the painful wounds of the past could be healed.

The older bee sighed a weary sigh. He saw the goodness of Deborah's heart. Deborah was gracious, like her mother and her grandmother before her. She reminded him very much of Queen Rosemary, who he had loved and served long ago. His hardened heart began to soften.

Elder Cranberry spoke gently to her for the first time, "Princess Deborah, thank you for having the courage to come here today. I have not always treated you with the same kindness you have shown me this morning, and I want to apologize for that. I would also like to ask your forgiveness for misleading your grandmother and the elders long ago and causing an end to singing in the colony. I allowed my grief to cloud my decisions. My foolish pride has prevented me from doing the right thing and asking for forgiveness until now. Please, would you forgive me?"

Deborah forgave him without hesitation and assured him of the forgiveness and understanding of the queen and her elders. It was time for everyone to move forward together in unity, instead of looking back at the losses and failures of the past.

Elder Cranberry agreed. Looking at the young princess, he spoke sincerely, "Deborah, I believe you have seeds of greatness within you to become a gifted teacher, and a great leader one day. You have honored me with your request for help. I will give you my answer before this day is over. I promise you that."

Her heart was full of hope for the future of the colony as she left his chamber that morning. Deborah had a feeling his answer would be yes, but even if it wasn't, she felt encouraged by the change in their relationship. Deborah was certain of one thing; everything was going to work out just the way it was supposed to now that singing was re-established in the colony.

As she made her way back to her room, the young princess felt an excitement about her role as the singing tutor. Her wings hummed loudly as she turned the next corner—and flew right into

Tadpole who was flying far too fast as usual.

"Ouch! Sorry Sis, are you okay? I went to your room first but you weren't there so I came to find you. Where have you been?" Tadpole said, picking himself up off the ground.

Deborah was too happy to be mad with her little brother for long, and she dusted herself off from the crash.

"Tadpole, you really need to slow down, you know. You're always in such a hurry! I've been talking to Elder Cranberry, but I'll tell you more about that later. Speaking with him got me thinking though; it's amazing how we think we know someone and judge them before we find out what they have been through. I think I'm going to really like Elder Cranberry after today."

Deborah saw her brother's puzzled look but decided to explain everything later. It was time to go have some fun together before work began in the meadows that afternoon.

"I tell you what, Tad, I'll race you to the honey store to grab a snack, then we can go to the—"

Before she had time to finish her sentence, Tadpole darted off ahead of her, yelling over his shoulder, "Last one there's a mosquito! Catch me if you can!"

She grinned and took off after him, shaking her head at her little brother's love for speed.

Princess Deborah had gained so much from her grand adventure at the Big River. She had taken a big risk leaving Bluebell Meadows in search of the golden flowers, and look what wonderful things had happened! She had made life-long friends in a new land and discovered she was a lot braver than she thought she was. The young princess and her companions had faced many dangers to finally rescue Uncle Albert from certain death. Having her uncle home again made facing those dangers worth it all.

The princess had learned that all great adventures have twists and turns, and unexpected things can happen—like singing with sunflowers! She would never forget the chorus of nature they sang together in the meadows, which in turn led to the return of singing in the colony. It was more than she could have ever hoped for or imagined!

Deborah was also learning that sometimes those around her have a painful story from their past, like Elder Cranberry. She knew that choosing to forgive his past mistakes would lead to freedom and change. She had also learned that how others appear on the outside might not reflect who they truly are on the inside. She knew in her heart that somehow this would lead her to having greater compassion and understanding for those in her care as future queen of the colony.

As she followed Tadpole to the honey store, Deborah was thankful for every lesson she was learning. Each one was forming the character she would need to one day rule and reign as the queen she was born to be.

And who knows, perhaps in the days ahead Princess Deborah would have the opportunity for more grand adventures with Kite at the Big River. She certainly hoped so! One thing was certain—because she had taken a risk, life in the colony would never be the same again.

~ THE END ~

FUN FACTS
About Honey Bees

Dear Reader,

I hope you enjoyed reading the story of Deborah and Kite's grand adventure at the Big River!

The honey bee is a very important creature to have in our world for many reasons. Not only are they cute and furry, but they play a vital role in providing food for the human race by pollinating our crops, such as apples, melons, blueberries, almonds, and cherries, causing them to reproduce.

Here is an amazing statement to show you how important honey bees are to human beings (see Honey Love website http://honeylove.org/bees/):

> "Bees pollinate 80% of the world's plants including 90 different food crops. 1 out of

every 3 or 4 bites of food you eat is thanks to bees!"

Wow! In my research for this book, I asked my friends at the Honey Bee Society if they would put together some fun facts for you so you could learn more about these fascinating and important pollinators. Here are ten amazing things to know about the humble honey bee:

> **1)** Did you know honey bees have hairy eyes? Actually, their entire body is covered in hair, which helps them to hold onto pollen while foraging!

> **2)** Honey bees actually have 5 eyes! Aside from their two main large eyes, they have 3 smaller ones on the top of their head which can detect movement and simple shapes.

3) A queen honey bee lays around 2,000 eggs a day and can live for several years!

4) There are three types of bees who live inside a hive; queen, workers, and drones.

5) Workers bees are all female and do all the work in the hive, whereas drones, male bees, just eat honey and hang out with other drones. What a life!

6) Over the course of her short thirty-day lifespan, a worker honey bee will only produce 1/12 a teaspoon of honey.

7) Depending on which type of flower a worker bee gathers nectar from will change the flavor of the resulting honey.

8) Honey bees can fly up to 20 miles per hour!

9) When worker bees find a patch of flowers they go back to the hive (a manmade structure to keep bees) and dance in front of the other bees to tell them about how to get there!

10) The inside of a beehive is always 93-95 F to keep the queen warm, which helps during the freezing cold winters.

If you would like to find out even more, please visit their website at **TheHoneyBeeSociety.org** or send them an email to **contact@TheHoneyBeeSociety.org**.

Ian from The Honey Bee Society told me they love teaching kids about honey bees, butterflies and lots of other pollinators. During the classroom visits children get to experience these pollinators up close and personal! They share about the importance of pollinators in the world and how children can help by planting more flowers.

He also said there is a simple way you can encourage honey bees into your neighborhood:

> *"An easy way to make a difference in your own backyard is to provide many different flowers which attract bees and other pollinators. Everyone is able to plant flowers and watch for the visiting butterflies and bees. Even a simple potted flower makes a difference for a honey bee!"*

Perhaps you and your friends would like to plant some sunflower seeds and watch them grow. You may attract a honey bee like Princess Deborah—you never know, you might even hear them singing together!

Gillian Blackah-Kingsley

(AUTHOR)

Gillian was born in the north of England, the daughter of journalist and newspaper editor, Michael Blackah. Her great-great-grandfather was a published poet from the Yorkshire mining community of the late 1800s. Gillian recently discovered a gift for writing poetry and is finding joy in continuing the legacy of writing in her family line. This book is her first children's novel. It is the first in a series of books she is writing about the adventures of Deborah and her friends.

Like Deborah, Gillian has always loved having adventures and discovering new places to visit. She and her lovely husband, Steve, enjoy traveling together and meeting new people. They live in a mountain community in southern California, close to the Kingsley kids, grandkids, and great-grandchildren.

Visit Gillian's website: GillianBlackah-Kingsley.com.

Nicola E. Hill
(ILLUSTRATOR)

Nicola delights in curating experiences that open doors for people to escape into moments of delight. Whether through color, texture, flavor, or design, in the kitchen, on a canvas, on the page, or in a garden, she desires to create feelings of joy and pleasure through everything her hands touch.

Digital art and illustration are a new adventure for her. Nicola grew up painting, drawing, and sculpting. She is an artist, chef, gardener, animal lover, mother, and wife, as well as a dreamer and visionary who lives to make the world a more beautiful place.